MISSION ECONOMY

MISSION ECONOMY

A Moonshot Guide to
Changing Capitalism

MARIANA MAZZUCATO

HARPER
BUSINESS
An Imprint of HarperCollins*Publishers*

HarperCollins books may be purchased for educational, business, or sales promotional use. For information, please email the Special Markets Department at SPsales@harpercollins.com.

Originally published in the United Kingdom in 2021 by Allen Lane.

FIRST U.S. EDITION

Library of Congress Cataloging-in-Publication Data

Names: Mazzucato, Mariana, 1968- author.
Title: Mission economy : a moonshot guide to changing capitalism / Mariana
  Mazzucato.
Description: New York : Harper Business, 2021. | Includes bibliographical
  references and index.
Identifiers: LCCN 2020058558 (print) | LCCN 2020058559 (ebook) | ISBN
  9780063046238 (hardcover) | ISBN 9780063046269 (ebook)
Subjects: LCSH: Economic policy. | Capitalism. | Business and politics. |
  Sustainable development. | Organizational change. | Organizational
  effectiveness.
Classification: LCC HD87.5 .M39 2021 (print) | LCC HD87.5 (ebook) | DDC
  330.12/2—dc23
LC record available at https://lccn.loc.gov/2020058558
LC ebook record available at https://lccn.loc.gov/2020058559

21 22 23 24 25   LSC   10 9 8 7 6 5 4 3 2

For all those who dedicate their lives to bringing public purpose and the common good to the centre of how we create value

Contents

List of Figures and Tables

Figures

Tables

Acknowledgements

Over the past several years, I have been lucky to work with policymakers who have interacted with me on many of the ideas in this book. The book is very much dedicated to them.

My ambition to rethink capitalism through rethinking the state began about a decade ago, when I started bringing together leaders from public organizations across the world to learn from each other – specifically, to better understand how to step outside the comfort zone of fixing market failures and into the ambitious, risk-taking world of making and shaping markets. These include leaders from organizations such as the Defense Advanced Research Projects Agency, Advanced Research Projects Agency – Energy, National Institutes of Health and NASA in the USA; the European Commission (EC) and the European Space Agency, the BBC, Government Digital Services and Innovate UK in the UK; the Chief Scientific Officer of Israel and Yozma in Israel; Vinnova in Sweden; Sitra in Finland; and different public banks like the KfW in Germany and BNDES in Brazil. What I found in all of my conversations with them was a real desire and thirst for a new framing of what public policy was about. It became clear that overcoming major technological and social challenges required a bold portfolio approach, a redesigning of tools like procurement and a proper economic theory to confront the directionality of growth head on. Engagement with them has enriched my understanding of the complexities of the 'real world' enormously.

My work also led me to set up the Institute for Innovation and Public Purpose (IIPP) at University College London (UCL). The objective was to replace a bilateral relationship with public organizations with a platform that could systematically explore how to 'do government' differently. At IIPP, my team and I are writing a new curriculum based on the premise that civil servants are not just market fixers but value co-creators and shapers. We are actively exploring questions such as: what value is being created, and is it good for people and the planet? How can we measure public value? What new participatory structures are needed to create an inclusive process while taking direction from democratically legitimate priorities, such as a green deal or a new way to understand the welfare state? We have worked with policymakers worldwide on transformative projects that inform our teaching and research – and vice versa – such as setting up a public bank in Scotland, rethinking innovation policy tools for the EC, and developing a carbon-neutral policy for the city of Manchester. Indeed, a siloed approach to academia has no place in learning how to do government differently. My thanks also to the senior leadership team across UCL: Provost Michael Arthur, David Price (Vice Provost for Research), and Alan Penn (ex-Dean of the Bartlett faculty) – who together not only hired me but also let me structure IIPP in a way that gives policy and practice as much weight as teaching and research, with the feedback between them our key goal.

I would also like to thank several leaders from the policy world who have worked diligently with me over the years and informed many of the insights in this book. This list includes Carlos Moedas, ex-commissioner for Directorate-General for Research, Science and Innovation in the EC, and who chose me as a personal advisor. Together with his team we managed to bring a missions instrument to EC legislation (a story I tell in Chapter 5). It also includes Nicola Sturgeon, First Minister of Scotland, who trusted me to work with her team to design a new mission-oriented public bank. It includes Greg Clarke in his role as Secretary of State for the Department of Business, Energy and Industrial Strategy in the UK government, who listened to me talk endlessly about why industrial strategy should not be sector-focused but challenge-focused – and then asked me to set up a commission on Mission-oriented Industrial Strategy, which I co-chaired with Lord Willetts (David) – a collaborator full of wisdom since his days as Minister of State for Universities and Science. Finally, it includes policymakers with whom I have recently started working closely: Cyril Ramaphosa, the President of South Africa, whose country faces great challenges, including those around state capacity, but whose energy and interest in new modes of economic models is as engaging as it is challenging; Giuseppe Conte, Italy's Prime Minister, who, in choosing me as a special advisor, allowed me to help structure Italy's post-COVID recovery plan using the missions approach as a framework for addressing the country's challenges around climate, health and digitalization; and Georgia Gould, leader of Camden Council, London, with whom I am embarking on a new adventure, the Camden Renewal Commission. The commission aims to use the missions approach to bring new participatory processes and governance models to Camden Council's economic plan. One member of the Commission, George Mpanga (otherwise known as George the Poet), has provided particular inspiration for me in the last year through his quest to make sure that big ideas about reforming our dysfunctional and unequal economy are nested in new forms of storytelling.

I would also like to thank Fr Augusto Zampini, who led the Vatican's post-COVID task force, and who, along with Pope Francis, has taught me much about the urgent need for a common good approach in economics.

I should note that the risk of working so closely with policy-makers is that sometimes your ideas get misinterpreted or are implemented incorrectly. As long as this is a learning-by-doing process, that is fine. Indeed, this book aims to help governments see themselves as learning organizations. I would like to thank my colleagues who read drafts of the book – some in its entirety, others helping with sections – and provided incredibly useful comments. These include my long-time mentor Carlota Perez (reminding me never to forget the big picture!), and the following colleagues in alphabetical order: Antonio Andreoni, Guendalina Anzolin, Rosie Collington, Brian Collins, Rowan Conway, George Dibb, Ryan Farrell, David Frayman, Simone Gasperin, Dan Hill, Rainer Kattel, Katie Kedward, Henry Li, Laurie Macfarlane, Giulio Quaggiotto, Josh Ryan-Collins and Asker Voldsgaard. I am also deeply grateful for the in-depth comments on the draft from Patrick Besha, Senior Policy Advisor at NASA and Robert Schroder from the EC.

As with my previous book, I benefited immensely from a close collaboration with Michael Prest, a journalist and editor who helped translate my ideas into easier language. Our long chats in the Lord Stanley pub (again!) were embedded with reflections of the challenges global governments are facing, and the much-needed steering of the ship. His charm, warmth and friendship were just as important as his careful edits.

The final stages of editing were helped by Rachel Farrell, a patient editor able to bring elegance and logic back to tangly passages. Her tireless ability to work days, nights and weekends, while raising a young family, allowed me to start Mondays feeling that the constant changes were progressing closer to the finishing line.

I was also lucky to convince my neighbour and long-time family friend in north London, Dennis Yandoli, to read the book with a critical eye, and contribute to the stories told through his passion for the moon landing. He often came to our meetings wearing an Apollo 13 or JFK T-shirt.

I would also like to thank my editor at Allen Lane/Penguin, Stuart Proffitt, whose careful editing and comments pushed the boundaries of the book. He played devil's advocate and also challenged me to make sure the book was as much about rethinking capitalism as it was about rethinking government. Warm thanks also the rest of the Penguin team: Etty Eastwood, Ania Gordon, Taryn Jones, Linden Lawson, Rebecca Lee and Alice Skinner. Sarah Chalfant, my agent at Wylie, and her excellent colleagues Ekin Oklap and Alba Ziegler-Bailey, helped me navigate the world of international publishers, while always finding the time to provide encouraging comments on articles, chapters and proposals.

Finally, I would like to thank my husband, Carlo Cresto-Dina, for always reminding me to reflect on the role of the cultural sector – and its centrality in creatively reimagining the life we want to lead. And I thank my children, Leon, Micol, Luce and Sofia, whose smiles, laughs, questions, playfulness and especially their deep empathy for all those around them make everything else secondary and worth the battle along the way.

Preface

As I write this book we are living through the COVID-19 pandemic, which poses massive challenges to every member of society around the world. Defeating the pandemic requires huge investments in physical and social goods and services – from the race to develop a vaccine or effective therapies, personal protective equipment (PPE) and appropriate methods of online learning for children not in school to new thinking about social safety nets. It also requires an unprecedented level of collaboration between nations, citizens, government and the private sector – the like of which we haven't seen in our lifetime. Fundamentally, it is a litmus test of state capacity and effective governance within and between countries.

Governments across the globe are adapting to this challenge in different ways and with different degrees of success. Governance is key to successful adaptation.[1] Countries' responses have differed in both the quantity and the quality of actions taken. Many governments have committed colossal sums with a 'whatever it takes' mentality. But if there is one thing we learned from the 2008 financial crisis, it is that injecting trillions into the economy will have little effect if the structures they are spent on are weak. We cannot risk that happening again.

Can we produce enough PPE for front-line workers? Enough ventilators for patients in intensive care units? A vaccine to help build immunity? Can we protect people who have lost their jobs so they have the basic right to a minimum income, food, shelter and education?

The answers to all these questions depend on the organization of our economy – more than just the amount of money being thrown at problems. It depends on the concrete structures, capacity and types of partnerships between the public and private sectors. It also requires the vision to imagine a different world. It is a vision for what kind of growth we want, plus the corresponding tools to get us that – that will create a new direction for the economy. And it is a new direction that is needed.

Vietnam's successful response to COVID-19 provides an interesting example. Although the country is still 'emerging' in terms of its developmental process, its government was able very quickly to spur the development of low-cost test kits. This was possible because it had the capability to mobilize different parts of society (academia, the army, the private sector, civil society) around a common goal and strategically use health research and development (R&D) procurement to 'crowd in' innovative solutions – that is, to use government spending to increase private-sector investment.[2] An effective public–private collaboration allowed for rapid commercialization of the kits, which were then exported to Europe and beyond, as well as deployed throughout Vietnam itself. The government was also able to galvanize poster artists, creatively harness social media and even produce stamps to promote behavioural change.[3] In India, the state of Kerala's success story (in contrast to a patchy national response) is also the result of long-term investment in health (including the protocols put in place after the 2018–19 outbreak of the Nipah virus, like COVID-19 a zoonotic virus) and a successful public–private partnership model between state medical services and private providers.[4] Bolstered by a high level of citizen trust built over the years, the machinery of government, complemented by self-help groups, was quick to put in place tight restriction measures while catering for the most vulnerable, including migrant workers.[5]

But in many parts of the world the picture has been much less rosy. As this book goes to press, the problems being faced by both the USA and the UK are the result of forty years of weakening ability to govern and manage – fuelled by the ideology that government needs to take a back seat and only come in to fix problems when they arise. A public management creed that belittles the ability of government to act effectively and promotes privatization has fostered much outsourcing of government capacity to the private sector and a relentless but misguided focus on static measures of efficiency,[6] leaving governments with fewer options and even latching onto unrealistic technology panaceas such as artificial intelligence or 'smart cities'. It has also led to lower investment in public capabilities, the loss of institutional memory and an increased dependence on consulting companies, which have benefited from billions in government contracts.

In the UK, the government outsourced health contracts worth £9.2 billion in 2018 alone.[7] Over 84 per cent of care home beds are in privately owned homes, and 50,000 of those are beds are in homes run by private equity companies whose ultimate aim is profit, not care. And this outsourcing has been combined with cuts in public investment. The total value of the public-health grant in the UK – which enables local authorities to provide vital health care and preventative services – has been declining in real terms, from £4 billion in 2015–16 to £3.2 billion in 2020/21, a decrease close to £900 million.[8] Year-on-year cuts to the grant only came to an end in 2020 when

COVID-19 was wreaking havoc, but the grant remained 22 per cent lower on a real-term per capita basis than in 2015–16.[9] By this time, the decline had already caused substantial damage to local public-health capacity and compromised the effectiveness of its response to COVID-19.[10]

And the mantra about greater efficiency is just that – a mantra. In the UK, when the international consultancy company Deloitte was paid to manage COVID-19 testing they lost the tests. This was a reminder of the massive failure of G4S, another private company picking up public contracts, to provide security for the 2012 London Olympics, which led to the military being called in to save the day. Similarly, Serco, a private company that consistently wins outsourcing contracts, was fined for its fraudulent use of electronic tagging for prisoners.[11] And yet it won a £45.8 million test-and-trace contract just one year after it was fined more than £1 million for failures including breaching data protection rules (in which it accidentally revealed the email addresses of trainees).

The US federal government suffered a similar fate. In 2007 it drew up a plan to spur the development of low-cost, portable ventilators for deployment in cases of emergency. By early 2020, a full thirteen years later, no ventilators had been delivered, substantially because of its reliance on outsourcing. The COVID-19 crisis has made the consequences of this lack of capacity all the more dramatic. Indeed, President Barack Obama's administration had already run into embarrassing IT problems in 2010 when it tried to roll out its health-care insurance reforms, the Patient Protection and Affordable Care Act – colloquially known as Obamacare. Many people could not access the site HealthCare.gov or complete their applications for insurance. A wave of bad publicity broke, which Obamacare's opponents exploited. Had there been more technology capacity within the US government itself it is likely the administration would have faced fewer difficulties and less political flak. And yet, not surprisingly, in both 2013 and 2018 Serco – shamed in the UK by its constant failures – won contracts with the US government to run the health insurance filing for Obamacare: $1.2 billion in 2013 and another $900 million in 2018.[12]

Outsourcing in itself is not a problem as long as governments remain capable, risk-prepared and have foresight; and as long as the underlying 'partnerships' with the private sector are truly designed in the public interest. The irony is that so much outsourcing has damaged governments' abilities to structure contracts. In March 2020, in an echo of the US government's difficulties, the UK government failed to secure the number of ventilators it thought it needed.[13]

A key lesson is that, in crises, government intervention is only effective if the state has the corresponding capability to act. Far from retrenching to the role of being at best fixers of market failure and at worst outsourcers, governments should invest in building their muscle in critical areas such as productive capacity, procurement capabilities, public-private collaborations that genuinely serve the public interest, and digital and data expertise (while safeguarding privacy and security). Without this, they cannot even devise robust terms of reference for the companies they bring in, which can then easily capture the agenda.[14]

This book argues that we have lost our way and cannot keep making the same mistakes. The world is facing an abundance of different challenges – from those related to health to those related to the climate crisis to those related to governing digital technology to protect privacy. Indeed, in 2015 193 countries signed a commitment to tackle seventeen ambitious UN Sustainable Development Goals (SDGs) by 2030 – covering problems ranging from poverty to polluted oceans. To address them, we need a very different approach to public-private partnerships from the one we have now. This requires a massive rethink of what government is for and the types of capability and capacity it needs. But, more importantly, it depends on what sort of capitalism we want to build, how to govern the relationships between the public and private sectors and how to structure rules, relationships and investments so that all people can flourish and planetary boundaries are respected. It is, as will be argued, about creating a solutions-based economy, focused on the most ambitious goals – the ones that really matter to people and to the planet. This is not about invoking the concept of a 'moonshot' as a siloed pet project. It is about transforming government from within and strengthening its systems – those for health, education, transport or the environment – while giving the economy a new direction.

To get back onto the right path we need to ask ourselves again what sort of role government should play in the economy, and consequentially the instruments, structures and capabilities it requires – both within public organizations but also to foster collaborations between public and private organizations that work together symbiotically – sharing both risks and rewards – to solve the most pressing problems of our time. In this sense it is about rethinking capitalism.

The challenges are urgent. The lives of people, and the health of the planet, depend on meeting them.

PART I: A MISSION GROUNDED

What stands in the way of the next moonshot

1: The Mission and Purpose

In September 1962 in a famous speech at Rice University, President John F. Kennedy announced that the US government would set out on 'the most hazardous and dangerous and greatest adventure on which man has ever embarked': landing a man on the moon and bringing him back safely. He declared the ambition to do it 'before this decade is out'.[1] The USA landed two men (yes, in the beginning it was just men) on the moon seven years later, on 20 July 1969.

When Kennedy spoke, the USA still lagged behind the USSR in space technology. In 1957, the USSR had stunned the world by launching Sputnik, the first artificial satellite to orbit the earth. As recently as April 1961, Yuri Gagarin had become the first human to orbit the earth in his capsule, *Vostok 1*. The Cold War was intense and there was deep concern that the Soviet Union had stolen a threatening technological and military march on the USA and the West. Kennedy had claimed in his 1960 election campaign that there was a 'missile gap' between the USA and the Soviet Union.[2] The claim was based on CIA and Pentagon estimates that the Soviet Union had more intercontinental ballistic missiles than the USA, but after Kennedy became president, it emerged that in fact the USA had more. The urge to beat the Russians, therefore, galvanized one of the most innovative feats in human history.

What became known as the Apollo programme cost the US government $28 billion, or $283 billion in 2020 dollars.[3] It took up 4 per cent of the US budget and involved over 400,000 workers in the National Aeronautics and Space Administration (NASA), universities and contractors. But cost was not the issue: the point was to get the job done. Indeed, Kennedy was not shy about talking about the expense, explicitly saying in his speech, 'all this costs us all a good deal of money.' Indeed, the space budget, he argued, was getting higher every year and stood in 1962 at about $5.4 billion a year: 'a staggering sum, though somewhat less than we pay for cigarettes and cigars every year'. And would it necessarily bring success? No, he was clear that the value for money was completely uncertain: 'I realize that this is in some measure an act of faith and vision, for we do not now know what benefits await us.'

What a contrast with how, today, we hear about *costs* of our public services – and the implication on annual deficits and debt – not the ambition or the grand outcomes they are trying to achieve. The assumption is that if we spend more in one area, we have to spend less in another. This could not be further from the approach to space exploration, when everyone's energy and attention was dedicated to the outcome – a successful moon landing – and the investment and innovation it demanded.

Kennedy foresaw the way in which the ambitious mission would result in 'spillovers' affecting life on earth – technological and organizational innovations that could never have been predicted at the beginning. Indeed, the technology needed to process data in real time and house that processing inside the lunar module's small computer is what stimulated much of the innovation behind what we today call software.[4] And new management methods emerged, too, that broke down large, complex problems into smaller packages. Later,

Boeing copied this model to build the 747, the world's first jumbo jet.

This book encourages us to apply the same level of boldness and experimentation to the biggest problems of our time – from health challenges such as pandemics, to environmental challenges such as global warming, to educational challenges such as the divide in opportunity and achievement between students partly caused by unequal access to digital technology. These 'wicked' problems require not just technological, but also social, organizational and political innovations. They are huge, complex and resistant to simple solutions. We must solve them – not merely accommodate them – by focusing policymaking on *outcomes*. And this means getting the public and private sectors to truly collaborate on investing in solutions, having a long-run view, and governing the process to make sure it is done in the public interest.

The moon landing was a massive exercise in problem-solving, with the public sector in the driving seat and working closely with companies – small, medium and large – on hundreds of individual problems. It required collaboration between government and many different sectors, from computing and electrical equipment to nutrition and materials. Government used its purchasing power to develop procurement contracts that were short, clear and massively ambitious. When the private sector sometimes failed to deliver, NASA threw back the challenge and did not pay until the solution was right. If successful, companies could grow through serving the new markets that government purchases opened up and scale up through a purpose-driven strategy.

What integrated all these efforts and gave them direction was that they were part of a mission – a mission led by government and achieved by many. Today, a 'mission-oriented' approach – partnerships between the public and private sectors aimed at solving key societal problems – is desperately needed. Imagine, for example, using public-sector procurement policy to stimulate as much innovation as possible – social, organizational and technological – to solve problems as diverse as knife crime in cities or loneliness of the elderly at home.

Of course, lessons from the moon landing cannot just be cut and pasted onto any challenge. But they do highlight the need to resurrect ambition and vision in our everyday policy-making. This cannot just be about bold statements. We have to believe in the public sector and invest in its core capabilities, including the ability to interact with other value creators in society, and design contracts that work in the public interest. We must create more effective interfaces with innovations across the whole of society; rethink how policies are designed; change how intellectual property regimes are governed; and use R&D to distribute intelligence across academia, government, business and civil society. This means restoring public purpose in policies so that they are aimed at creating tangible benefits for citizens and setting goals that matter to people – driven by public-interest considerations rather than profit.[5] It also means placing purpose at the core of corporate governance and considering the needs of all stakeholders, including workers and community institutions, as opposed to just shareholders (owners of stock in a company).

In this context, 'moonshot' thinking is about setting targets that are ambitious but also inspirational, able to catalyse innovation across multiple sectors and actors in the economy. It is about imagining a better future and organizing public and

6

private investments to achieve that future. This, in the end, is what got a man on the moon and back.

But there is a catch.

Conventional wisdom continues to portray government as a clunky bureaucratic machine that cannot innovate: at best, its role is to fix, regulate, redistribute; it corrects markets when they go wrong. According to this view, civil servants are not as creative and risk-taking as the entrepreneurs of Silicon Valley, and government should simply level the playing field and then get out of the way – so the risk-takers in private business can play the game.

This book's thesis is that we cannot move on from the key problems facing our economies until we abandon this narrow view. Mission thinking of the kind I outline here can help us restructure contemporary capitalism. The scale of the reinvention calls for a new narrative and new vocabulary for our political economy, using the idea of public purpose to guide policy and business activity.[6] This requires ambition – making sure that the contracts, relationships and messaging result in a more sustainable and just society. And it requires a process that is as inclusive as possible, involving many value creators. Public purpose must lie at the centre of how wealth is created collectively to bring stronger alignment between value creation and value distribution. And the latter should not only be about *redistribution* (*ex post*) but also *predistribution* *ex ante*: a more symbiotic way for economic actors to relate, collaborate and share.

It is essential to link the micro properties of the system – such as how organizations are governed – to the macro patterns of the type of growth desired. By rethinking how the relationships between the public sector and private sector can be better governed around public purpose, we can create growth that is better balanced and resilient, with new capabilities and opportunities spread across the economy. But this means, at the start, replacing the fashionable, bland terminology of 'partnership' with clearer metrics as to what a symbiotic and mutualistic ecosystem looks like; that is, one in which risks and rewards are more equally shared. In our era, unfortunately, the relationship is often parasitic: public-health funding is structured so that publicly financed drugs are too expensive for citizens to buy.

I call this different way of doing things a mission-oriented approach. It means choosing directions for the economy and then putting the problems that need solving to get there at the centre of how we design our economic system. It means designing policies that catalyse investment, innovation and collaboration across a wide variety of actors in the economy, engaging both business and citizens. It means asking what kind of markets we want, rather than what problem in the market needs to be fixed. It means using instruments such as loans, grants and procurement to drive the most innovative solutions to tackle specific problems, whether those be getting plastic out of the ocean or narrowing the digital divide. The wrong question is: how much money is there and what can we do with it? The right question is: what needs doing and how can we structure budgets to meet those goals?

This is a huge task. We live in an era in which capitalism is in crisis and a flawed ideology about the role of government has infiltrated our expectations of what it can do – and thus what other actors can do in partnership with government. But a time of crisis is exactly the moment to reimagine what type of society we want to build, and the capabilities and capacities we need to get us there.

Is this book about rethinking government or rethinking capitalism? The answer is, both. Changing capitalism means changing both how government is structured and how business is run – and how public and private organizations interrelate. Driving governance structures of organizations, and relationships between organizations, through a notion of 'purpose' is the key to a mission-oriented approach.

Indeed, for many years there have been calls for corporate governance modes to be more 'purposeful' and move away from shareholder capitalism to stakeholder capitalism. In January 2018 Larry Fink, the CEO of BlackRock, wrote a letter to 500 CEOs called 'A Sense of Purpose'. In it he argued: 'Without a sense of purpose, no company, either public or private, can achieve its full potential. It will ultimately lose the license to operate from key stakeholders. It will succumb to short-term pressures to distribute earnings, and, in the process, sacrifice investments in employee development, innovation, and capital expenditures that are necessary for long-term growth.'[7] A year and a half later, in August 2019, the same message was echoed by the Business Roundtable, a club of 180 powerful CEOs including those of Apple, Accenture and JPMorgan Chase. In a statement, its members argued that to foster a more functional form of capitalism, profits had to be more widely distributed to all stakeholders, including workers and communities – the key stakeholders.[8]

The problem is that, notwithstanding these calls for change, not much *is* changing. This is not only because the change needed must go to the very core of business models and value chains, instead of being treated as an afterthought;

it is also because a renewed sense of purpose must go to the centre of the relationship between organizations in the economy, not just inside business. Change comes from reimagining *how* different organizations and actors in the economy co-create value. Yes, this book does focus on much-needed changes in our public institutions. But because government activity – direct investments, indirect subsidies, tax and regulations – lies at the centre of nearly all relationships, rethinking government means rethinking capitalism.

While this book is intended for both theorists and practitioners, it is meant especially as a guide to how we can 'do' capitalism differently. It argues that we should change organizations, governance structures and the design of the practical levers of economic policy – the tools we need to build a purpose-oriented economy.

2: Capitalism in Crisis

Even before the COVID-19 pandemic hit in 2020, capitalism was stuck. It had – and has – no answers to a host of problems, perhaps most crucially the environmental crisis. From global heating to biodiversity loss, human activity is eroding the conditions necessary for social and environmental stability.[1] Under current mitigation policy commitments, global surface temperatures are on track to increase by over 3°C relative to pre-industrial times – a magnitude that is widely accepted to have catastrophic outcomes.[2] Species extinction has increased 100 to 1,000 times the background extinction rate, leading some scientists to announce that we are witnessing the sixth mass-extinction event.[3]

Rather than having a sustainable growth path, capitalism has built economies that inflated speculative bubbles, enriched the already immensely wealthy 1 per cent and were destroying the planet. In many Western and Western-style capitalist economies, real earnings for all but a few have barely risen in more than a decade – in some cases, such as the USA, in several decades – exacerbating inequalities between groups and regions despite high levels of employment.[4] The dynamics of inequality explain why the profits-to-wages ratio has reached record highs. Between 1995 and 2013, real median wages in Organization for Economic Co-operation and Development (OECD) countries grew at an annual average rate of 0.8 per cent versus 1.5 per cent growth in labour productivity.[5] In the period 1979–2018, real wages for the 50th and 10th percentiles of the wage distribution stagnated: there was 6.1 per cent cumulative real wage change over the whole period for the 50th percentile, 1.6 per cent for 10th percentile – versus 37.6 per cent for 90th percentile. In rich countries, private wealth-to-income ratios increased from 200–300 per cent in 1970 to 400–600 per cent in 2010.[6]

These economies were also, after 2008, hooked on the drug of quantitative easing – central banks injecting massive amounts of liquidity into the system – although economic growth and productivity improvement remained weak.[7] Personal debt was back to levels last seen in the early years of this century. By 2018, private debt to GDP reached 150 per cent in the USA, 170 per cent in the UK, 200 per cent in France and 207 per cent in China – all substantially higher than levels at the turn of the century.[8]

And much of business has been plagued by a dangerous combination of low investment, short-term management and high rewards to shareholders and company bosses.[9] In advanced economies, business investment has barely recovered to 2008 levels.[10] In the UK in the 1980s, typical CEO pay was twenty times higher than that of the average worker. By 2016, the average FTSE 100 CEO's pay was 129 times greater than that of the average employee.[11] Since 1980, UK dividend pay-out ratios have remained constant, irrespective of profitability. Share buybacks have increased in importance, consistently exceeding UK share issuance over the past decade. In the USA, total pay-outs to shareholders have come to almost $1 trillion, equalling pre-crisis peaks, increasing from around 10 per cent of internal cash flow in the 1970s to 60 per cent by 2015.[12]

And difficulties are also being experienced in authoritarian, state-capitalist societies. Today, China, the leading authoritarian economy, remains weighed down by inefficient and heavily indebted state industries, a banking system with huge 'zombie' loans, an ageing population, and the massive task of shifting the economy away from excessive export dependency and towards greater domestic consumption. To be fair, it is making progress, and has real ambition about greening its economy, with over $1.7 trillion being invested as part of its five-year plan. But a central planning model is not likely to be one that will be able to take on the bold reforms to public and private collaboration that this book envisages.

The COVID-19 crisis also revealed just how fragile capitalism really is. People working in the gig economy have no security. High levels of corporate debt – partly taken on to pay dividends, buy back companies' own shares and indirectly boost senior executive pay – have left many companies with little to fall back on. Their strategy of relying on attenuated global supply chains to cut costs and reduce the bargaining power of their on-site workers proved to be an Achilles heel when the pandemic disrupted production globally and created fierce competition for even basic items, such as face masks. Some governments, particularly those of the UK and the USA, had outsourced so much of their capacity to the private sector and consultancies that they were not able to manage the crisis properly. This led to deadly blunders, as governments faced shortages in basic PPE and failed to set up enough testing for their populations.[13] The ultimate irony was that governments long wedded to austerity abruptly switched their affections to public spending, borrowing and creating deficits on a scale that would earlier have caused ideological apoplexy, as they struggled to do 'whatever it takes' to keep their national economies alive. Hammered under the twin blows of a collapse in output and a collapse in demand – largely induced by the government to suppress the virus – the Thatcher–Reagan model of the economy and society has broken down, and the global economy is wrestling with an historically severe depression.

A sluggish global economy, which spells particular disaster for developing countries and the less well-off in developed countries, has exacerbated social and political tensions that have been intensifying for decades. For far too many people, life feels precarious, either because they are in debt or their savings at most cover one month of rent.[14] Even in the USA, the world's biggest economy, whose working class was once a byword for prosperity, a report found that nearly three in ten adults would need to borrow money or sell something to cover a $400 unexpected expense.[15]

The balance of power has shifted away from workers and towards employers – for example, the relationship between an Uber driver and Uber as a multinational corporation is deliberately designed to shift risk from company to worker – and this, along with other cost-cutting practices that have reduced labour's negotiating power, is one of the reasons why the ratio of profits to wages has reached a record high in the last decade.[16] Others live hand to mouth on zero-hour contracts. Even when they have regular work, many people still depend on welfare to make ends meet.[17] Yet it is the low-paid and disregarded workers – garbage collectors, postal staff, hospital cleaners, care workers, bus drivers – upon whom society came to depend most during the COVID-19 crisis, not corporate bosses, financiers and residents of tax havens.

Long-standing political rifts have grown wider: between

nationalism and internationalism, democracy and autocracy, efficient and inefficient governments. A deep sense of injustice, powerlessness and distrust of elites – especially business and political elites – has eroded faith in democratic institutions. The global, multilateral system painfully constructed after World War Two and the broadly liberal, open values it embodies are under unprecedented strain. National salvation has trumped international co-operation, much to the delight of 'strongmen', demagogues and authoritarian regimes who can ride a tide of populism and exploit a climate of fear. To add to all of this, governments have continued to procrastinate in properly tackling the climate emergency. We can do better. But to do better, we need to fully understand how we got into the mess we are in.

To grasp the true scale of this challenge, it is important to understand that the issues described above are the *consequences* of deeper forces that together have led to a dysfunctional form of capitalism. There are (at least) four key sources of the problem: (1) the short-termism of the financial sector, (2) the financialization of business, (3) the climate emergency, and (4) slow or absent governments. In each, the way that organizations are structured and how they relate to each other are part of the problem. Their restructuring must, therefore, be part of the solution.

Finance is financing FIRE

The first problem is that the financial sector has largely been financing itself. Most finance goes back into finance, insurance and real estate rather than into productive uses. The acronym for this is FIRE (finance, insurance, real estate) – appropriate in the sense that it is burning the foundations on which long-term economic growth rests. In the USA and the UK, only about a fifth of finance goes into the productive economy (such as companies that want to innovate, infrastructure that needs building). And in the UK, 10 per cent of all UK bank lending helps non-financial firms; the rest supports real estate and financial assets.[18] In 1970 real estate lending constituted about 35 per cent of all bank lending in advanced economies; by 2007 the figure had risen to about 60 per cent.[19] The current structure of finance thus fuels a debt-driven system and speculative bubbles which, when they burst, bring banks and others begging for government bailouts. Some of these institutions are deemed 'too big to fail', as were banks in the 2008–9 financial crisis: if they failed, the entire system would come crashing down with them. So the banks got the bailouts: FIRE profits are private; FIRE losses are public. Bailing out the banks involved 'moral hazard' because, being judged too important to fail, they lived with an implicit government guarantee which tempted them to take excessive risks without having fully to face the consequences if their bets went wrong.

Business is focusing on quarterly returns

The second problem is that business itself has become financialized. In recent decades, finance has generally grown faster than the economy and, within non-financial sectors, financial activities and their accompanying attitudes have come to dominate business. An ever greater share of corporate profits has been used to boost short-term gains in stock prices rather than provide long-term investment in areas like new capital equipment, R&D and worker training: skills are insufficiently developed, too many jobs are 'McJobs' and insecure, and wages stay low.[20] Indeed, one of the reasons for the high level of private debt in the USA and the UK – driven by a form of capitalism that is aimed at maximizing the returns to shareholders, not all stakeholders – is that many workers need to take on debt to maintain their living standards but cannot earn enough to reduce or pay it off.[21] But, unfortunately, the problem goes even further in Scandinavia, where deregulation of the financial sector has also led to a rise in private debt (also due to home equity withdrawal-based consumption) and overinvestment in FIRE sectors.[22]

By purchasing its own shares, a corporation can artificially boost its stock price and that of its executives, who are paid in these stocks. In just the ten years to 2019, total buybacks by the Fortune 500 (an annual list of the 500 biggest US companies compiled by *Fortune* magazine, measured by revenues) exceeded nearly $4 trillion, with many companies spending over 100 per cent of their net income on a combination of buybacks and dividend pay-outs, thus raiding their capital reserves. Over the same period, six of America's biggest airlines spent an average of 96 per cent of their free cash flow on stock buybacks – the aircraft manufacturer Boeing spent 74 per cent of its free cash flow on stock buybacks – which didn't deter these companies from asking for federal government help when the COVID-19 crisis struck.[23]

The excuse often heard from business for doing this is that there are no 'opportunities for investment'. But, given that the greatest buybackers are in industries where opportunities clearly exist – pharmaceuticals and energy – this is unconvincing. Are there really no opportunities for innovation in antibiotics or treatments for tropical diseases that mostly affect poor people in developing countries, not to mention vaccines? (This question became particularly pertinent with the arrival of COVID-19.) Are there really no opportunities for aircraft manufacturers to invest in renewable energy and other green technologies? The chief culprit is a form of corporate governance obsessed with 'maximization of shareholder value' – essentially, maximizing stock prices. Even Jack Welch, the late CEO of General Electric, one of America's biggest companies, later in life called shareholder value 'the dumbest idea in the world'. He explained: 'Shareholder value is a result, not a strategy . . . Your main constituencies are your employees, your customers and your products. Managers and investors should not set share price increases as their overarching goal . . . Short-term profits should be allied with an increase in the long-term value of a company.'[24]

In practice, maximizing shareholder value has often involved loading companies with debt – a supposedly efficient model which leverages a company's capital base – with the risk that the company is dangerously exposed to unexpected turns of events, such as a pandemic or a market downturn. In 2017, for example, the USA suffered a severe retail slump. The long-established US retailer Toys 'R' Us went into liquidation. It had been acquired in 2005 by two private equity firms, Bain Capital and Kohlberg Kravis Roberts, and a real estate firm, Vornado Realty Trust. To buy the company they used the usual private equity formula, saddling it with debt to increase the return later.[25] Indeed, company debt rose soon after the takeover from $1.86 billion to nearly $5 billion. By

2007 debt interest payments were 97 per cent of the company's operating profit. The retail slump of the following years was severe, but the high debt burden imposed on Toys 'R' Us impaired its ability to adapt and increased its vulnerability to the downturn.[26] The excessive financialization of companies and remorseless pursuit of shareholder value has left many other major companies open to similar charges of moral hazard: ingenious financial structures benefit owners more than other stakeholders such as workers, suppliers and customers – let alone the wider communities in which companies operate.

The planet is warming

And third is a problem that dwarfs the others if not solved soon: the climate emergency, which will dramatically change life for humans, animals and plants on our planet. The 2019 Intergovernmental Panel on Climate Change report argues that we have just ten years left until climate breakdown is irreversible.[27] COVID-19 made us even more aware of the fragility of our environment and an economic system that depends on it. The climate emergency is very much a result of the four other problems in finance and business: fossil fuels still dominate our energy sources, industries are too carbon-intensive, the financial sector has fed the fossil-fuel-driven economy, and government is nurturing this dysfunctionality – in 2019, extraordinarily, subsidies to fossil-fuel companies were estimated at $20 billion a year in the USA and an enormous €55 billion a year in the European Union (EU).[28] Of the COVID-19 recovery funding allocated to energy companies by G20 governments, 56 per cent has been handed to fossil-fuel

projects, equivalent to $151bn (£119bn).[29] And when it comes
the mass extinction of animals and plants – the other great
(and related) environmental crisis – even less is being done.

Governments are tinkering, not leading

The only way to solve these problems is for governments to
address them proactively. And this brings us to the fourth
problem: governments have bought into the ideology that
their role is simply to fix problems, not achieve bold objectives. Mainstream economic theory does not view public
actors as creators and shapers, nor does it view markets as
serving a purpose that needs to be shaped. Rather, the current
ideology assumes that capitalism works through a 'market
mechanism' that is driven by the natural tendency for individuals to pursue their own self-interest, each maximizing
his/her own objective function: consumers maximize their
utility, workers maximize their preferences between leisure
and work, and companies maximize their profits. The story
goes on to say that when markets that emerge from these individual decisions fail to produce 'efficient' outcomes, the
government must step in – either correcting for positive externalities (like basic research) or negative externalities (like
pollution).

This book will argue that markets are not outcomes of
individual decision-making but of how each value-creating
actor is governed – including government itself. In this sense,
markets are 'embedded' in rules, norms and contracts affecting organizational behaviour, interactions and institutional
designs.[30] Government thus cannot limit itself to reactively

fixing markets, but must explicitly co-shape markets to deliver the outcomes society needs. It can and should guide the direction of the economy, serve as an 'investor of first resort' and take risks. It can and should shape markets to fulfil a purpose.

To a certain extent, government is already doing this; it's just happening in a random and piecemeal fashion. And the point is not a normative one – even deregulation provides a direction that a government might choose to give. The question is how to design tools that explicitly help achieve directionality with a purpose. Many government actions enable markets to function, or create and/or shape markets through investment in areas like education, research and physical infrastructure; demand generation through procurement; legal codes; and antitrust policies. In this sense, markets are embedded in institutions and norms and are co-created by different actors in both the public and private sectors, as well as by civil-society organizations such as trade unions. But the prevailing ideology either denies this role (for example, banks do not like to be reminded that they operate with an implicit government guarantee) or argues that government should not be acting in this way.

As a result, governments focus on fixing things when they go wrong, rather than on improving the everyday lives of citizens in imaginative ways. In fact, improvement and imagination are notable by their absence, slowness or rigidity. President Obama was right when he said in January 2012 that current methods of government are unfit for the twenty-first century because the most recent major innovations in government, such as how its departments are structured, occurred in the age of black-and-white TV.[31] Obama wanted to streamline the federal government to better support America's economy in an age of global competition.

Part of what's stopping civil servants from innovating is the fear of doing anything more than putting patches on the system when it starts malfunctioning. Ronald Reagan summed it up when he famously said: 'The nine most terrifying words in the English language are: "I'm from the government, and I'm here to help." '[32] Reagan echoed the sentiment of the nineteenth-century 'night watchman' state without understanding that it creates a self-fulfilling prophecy whereby government does too little, too late. It is always reacting and making running repairs to a sputtering system, like someone constantly patching a worn tyre rather than replacing it with a new one, slowly squandering its capacity to be an active value creator. And the patches have been big, from bailing out the banks to investing where the private sector refuses to put its money. Even 'public goods', such as spending to clean the air or to invest in new knowledge, are framed as corrections to markets rather than as true objectives. The problem is not 'big government' or 'small government'. The problem is the *type* of government: what it does and how.

None of the difficulties we are suffering are inevitable. They are a result of how we have chosen to govern our system. There is nothing in the stars that compels the financial sector to fail to invest in the real economy, or to invest only with short-term profit objectives. We have rewarded it for doing so – for example by reducing taxes on capital gains, by allowing interest payments on debt to be offset against corporate taxes, by permitting investment banking and retail banking to operate within the same corporate group and by wholesale deregulation.[33] There is nothing inevitable that makes an over-financialized business sector focus excessively on the short term. There is nothing inevitable about the public sector always being in reactive mode. And there is nothing inevitable about our planet continuing to warm, rendering it increasingly hostile to humans, plants and animals. These are choices that we collectively make. We have not demanded that the private sector does otherwise — even as a condition for accessing key public investments critical for private-sector profits, such as the $40 billion a year in publicly funded health innovation in the USA. The public sector has shown too little regard for voters' concerns about clean air, robust public-health systems, the regulation of business and planetary health.

The case for radical change is thus overwhelming. But to drive this change, we have to see the problem through a particular lens — concentrating on rethinking government in order to stimulate improvements across the economy. Why? The reason is simple: only government has the capacity to steer the transformation on the scale needed — to recast the way in which economic organizations are governed, how their relationships are structured and how economic actors and civil society relate to each other.

Indeed, rethinking corporate governance must be high on the agenda too. We have to shift business from focusing only on maximizing shareholder value to being driven by a range of stakeholders. Traditional corporate social responsibility is too limited to bring about this transformation. What's needed is clarity about what value is being created in the first place and a new way of working along the entire value chain to produce it. A revitalized sense of purpose is required across both government and business and how they work together. For example, it is possible for government activity to be structured in a way that rewards types of corporate behaviour that move us towards achieving sustainability targets. Such goals cannot be tackled simply by changes to corporate governance – through metrics like ESG (environmental social and corporate governance). They also require a fundamentally different way for business and the state to interact. If, for example, businesses' access to public subsidies was conditional on their meeting social and environmental targets, 'purpose' would also be embedded in contracts and inter-relationships.

Mission Economy is about how government must change from within in order to deliver on ambitious outcomes, as well as how it must change its interaction with other actors. The current state of the typical instruments used by governments, such as taxation, fiscal policy and monetary policy, is rudderless. There is no systemic directionality towards de-financialization or sustainability. No attempt to change the relative cost structure through the tax system and other instruments to gear investment towards eliminating waste, reducing materials and energy use and pollution. Why are we not seriously taxing the environmental 'bads' and favouring 'green'? Why are capital gains taxed less than income from work? Why is there no clear benefit for investing long-term rather than short-term? Why is nothing done to stop doubtfully legal high-frequency trading as well as the harmful practice of excessive share buybacks?[34] Why no attempt to redesign the welfare state to respond to the new conditions created by the digital technologies? There is no clear direction; unless letting the market do as it pleases regardless of results is a 'direction'. But, once a proper direction is systemically applied to the whole range of policies, leading to synergies in innovation and investment behaviour across the economy, government needs to do much more. It must transform *itself* into an innovating organization with the capacity and capability to energize and catalyse the economy to be more purpose-driven.

The first step is to unpick and map more precisely why governments have become so stuck. It is impossible to get better policies without first understanding the myths underlying bad policies, and the ideas needed to move forward.

3: Bad Theory, Bad Practice: Five Myths that Impede Progress

Since the 1980s, a mindset of aversion to risk has filled civil servants with the fear of doing anything more than facilitating the private sector. Risk-taking is not supposed to be part of their job description. Indeed, we often hear that government does not know how to invest and should never use its resources to set a direction for change, let alone dare to 'pick winners'. Although the governments of many countries have spent staggering amounts to keep their economies on life support during both the financial crisis and, more recently, the health pandemic, the neo-liberal economics which took hold in the Thatcher–Reagan era continue heavily to influence thinking, which still portrays governments as clunky, bureaucratic machines that suppress the animal spirits of the wealth-creating private sector – no matter how much the latter are bailed out crisis after crisis. These problematic theories about government lead to problematic practices that, for a variety of reasons, get in the way of a mission-oriented approach. Indeed, they put governments in the position of picking up the mess – whether through bailouts or redistributional policies – instead of shaping our economies to create wealth differently so our societies are more resilient, inclusive and sustainable in the first place.

This link between theory and practice is exactly what the great economist John Maynard Keynes meant when he said: 'Practical men, who believe themselves to be quite exempt from any intellectual influences, are usually the slaves of some defunct economist. Madmen in authority, who hear voices in the air, are distilling their frenzy from some academic scribbler of a few years back.[1] Below, I debunk five of the most common myths about government and explain why they're problematic for a mission-oriented approach to changing capitalism.

Myth 1: Businesses create value and take risks; governments only de-risk and facilitate

A fundamental assumption in common perception – but also nested deep in economic theory – is that value is uniquely created inside business. Government's job is to set the rules of the game, regulate, redistribute and fix market failures. Even central banks are seen in conventional theory as simply 'lenders of last resort', despite the fact that they prevented the entire financial system from falling apart after the 2008 financial crisis.

The result is that, in many areas, public institutions have lost the confidence to act. Even more important, they have lost the capability to act. If the public sector is not seen as a value creator, then it does not need to invest in its own capabilities, including strategic management, decision science and organizational behaviour – though even universities (not always considered models of efficiency) teach these subjects to managers. Indeed, rather than finding ways to work actively with business on public problems, the public sector has ended up frequently privatizing undertakings and outsourcing public contracts, hoping to save public money in the often mistaken belief that the private sector is more efficient, when in reality its aim is profit. Far from achieving its aims, this ideology of privatization and outsourcing has led to high costs, poor service, capture of government contracts by a small number of firms, and contracts that often leave taxpayers with risks they thought had been transferred to private firms, as discussed below in Myth 4, and that socialize risks while privatizing rewards.

The other side of that ideological coin is the belief that only business creates value. Here, risk-taking entrepreneurs, driven by the motive of profit, deserve a special place in society because only they, in the end, generate the tax revenues on which government depends, push innovation forward and create jobs. But the truth is not that simple. How private firms create value has been analysed extensively in the field of microeconomics, and its equivalent in business literature. There is no question that businesses create value and need to make profits, and should be free to do so. The issue is understanding *how* this occurs. Economics talks about the 'production function'. It explains how value is created within the firm (the microeconomic theory of value) by combining capital (tangible, such as machinery, and intangible, such as knowledge) with labour and technology.[2] In business studies, value is understood as being created inside the company by bringing together managerial expertise, strategic thinking and a dynamic (changing with circumstances) division of labour between workers.[3]

All this ignores the massive role of government in creating value, and taking risk in the process. In *The Entrepreneurial State* I argued that Silicon Valley itself is an outcome of such high-risk investments by the state, willing to take risks in the early stages of development of high-risk technologies which the private sector usually shies away from.[4] This is the case with the investments that led to the internet, where a critical role was played by DARPA, the Defence Advanced Research Projects Agency inside the US Department of Defense – and also by CERN in Europe with its invention of the World Wide Web. Indeed, not only the internet but nearly every other technology that makes our smart products smart was funded by public actors, such as GPS (funded by the US Navy), Siri (also funded by DARPA) and touch-screen display (funded initially by the CIA). It is also true of the high-risk, early-stage investments made in the pharmaceutical industry by public actors like the National Institutes of Health (NIH) – without which most blockbuster drugs would not have been developed. And the renewable energy industry has been greatly aided by investments made by public banks like the European Investment Bank or the KfW in Germany, with private finance often too risk-averse and focused on short-term returns.[5] On the demand side, it required organizations such as the Small Business Innovation Research Programme (SBIR), housed in the US Department of Commerce, to create markets for small and medium-sized enterprises (SMEs) by designing procurement policy so it is focused on helping SMEs provide goods and services via department budgets (about 3 per cent of the budget).

Globally, the actions of public agencies across the entire innovation chain have also been crucial, allowing innovation powerhouses to emerge: in Taiwan, the role of the Industrial Technology Research Institute; in Israel, that of the Office of the Chief Scientist; in Japan, the Ministry of International Trade and Industry; and in Singapore, the Agency for

Science, Technology and Research.[6] The Republic of Korea has been especially successful in developing electronics. It first made its entrance into the semiconductor industry in the 1970s, when it attracted US companies looking for cheap assembling facilities, and spent the following decade implementing widespread industrial policy measures that included supporting business groups capable of mass production and exporting consumer electronics. This led to the launch of the first commercial dynamic RAM product in 1984.[7]

In all of these cases, without ambitious public investment the private sector would have proved unwilling to invest in areas where the required funding was large, long-term and highly uncertain. Only after the risk had been absorbed by the public sector did private businesses take advantage of the new opportunities created by the innovation. Thus, the empirical evidence paints a very different picture from the theory based on highly dubious assumptions.

Myth 2: The purpose of government is to fix market failures

By ignoring the possibility that government can contribute to value creation, economic theory also assumes that markets can only be fixed, not created, by government policy. Markets may fail due to information asymmetries (such as when buyers and sellers do not have the same information), or positive externalities (such as funding public goods, basic research or public health) or negative externalities (such as pollution). In the case of the latter, government needs to step in with a policy such as a carbon tax – 'make the polluter pay'. In addition, government can also redistribute value, or wealth, through taxation. In macroeconomics (the study of the economy as a whole), the theory of taxation is central to understanding redistribution of value and focuses public action on making existing systems more efficient rather than transforming them.

Market failure theory (MFT) – the idea that public policy can at best fix market failures – has its origins in neoclassical 'welfare economics', the study of how economic decisions produce the well-being of society at large. MFT's starting point is the so-called first fundamental theorem (FFT) of welfare economics.[8] The theorem states that markets are the most efficient allocators of resources under three specific conditions: one, there is a complete set of markets, so that all goods and services supplied and demanded are traded at publicly known prices; two, all consumers and producers behave competitively; and three, an equilibrium exists (the forces of change in opposing directions are balanced – for example, the demand for bananas exactly matches the supply at a given price). Under these three conditions, the allocation of resources by markets is optimal in the way described by the economist Vilfredo Pareto: no other allocation will make a consumer or producer better off without making someone else worse off. Government, therefore, has no role at all in value creation.

According to MFT, violation of any of the three assumptions leads to inefficient allocation of resources by markets – market failures. If markets are not Pareto-efficient, then everyone could be made better off by public policies that correct the market failure. MFT suggests that governments intervene when the market fails due to positive externalities, negative externalities and information asymmetries. Sometimes, government can do things that are in the interests of the whole community: for example, it can provide mass vaccination to control polio, or free education for all. This public good is a positive externality. But according to MFT, to justify such an action government must provide what the private sector does not or cannot. In the case of negative externalities, government must devise market mechanisms to internalize external costs.

In addition to all this, in the 1960s and 1970s a new theory emerged in advanced economies which cast doubt on *any* government market-fixing and effectively argued for an even more limited government role: that government failure is even more dangerous than market failure. It was called public choice theory and it attempted to apply neoclassical welfare economics to political decision-making. Public choice theory looks at how the actions of agents (voters, bureaucrats, politicians) involved in policy could be considered from an economic-efficiency perspective. It assumes that agents, including government ones, are self-interested in the same way that private-market actors are assumed to be in neoclassical theory.[9] While in markets competition and the profit motive tend to enforce efficient choices, in collective decision-making processes in politics and public administration, according to public choice theory, the same discipline is absent. Policymaking is therefore considered to be subject to capture by interest groups, in particular those most able to influence policymakers because they have power or money. Capture might involve nepotism, cronyism, corruption, rent-seeking (making excessive profits, as from a winning a monopoly), misallocation of resources (backing ailing companies or 'picking losers') or unfair and damaging competition with private initiatives (crowding out). Capture by special

interests is all the more possible, it is argued, because collective action by voters tends to be weak. Rational voters have
little reason to take an interest in political decisions since most
of these have only a tiny impact on their lives. In public
administration, the lack of competitive pressures leads to
'bureau-maximizing' behaviour, whereby departments and
agencies look after their own survival rather than the 'common
good'.

If that is true, government intervention will not necessarily result in a more efficient outcome even where market failure
is clear. Rather, there could also be 'government failure'. For
example, decisions aimed at improving welfare could make
things even worse than they would have been under market
failure.[10] By this approach, market failure is a necessary but
not sufficient condition for governmental intervention; it is
sufficient only if the gains from intervention outweigh the
losses from government failure.[11] From this perspective, there
is a trade-off between two inefficient outcomes – one generated by free markets (market failure) and the other by
government intervention (government failure). Some economists suggest the solution lies in correcting failures such as
imperfect information.[12] Others, especially public-choice
advocates, argue for leaving resource allocation to markets
(which may be able to correct their failures on their own), or the
creation of market-type discipline within public agencies.[13]

But just as MFT is a theoretical construct, so is its alter ego,
public choice theory. The axiom underlying public choice
theory is that bureaucrats and politicians behave like free-
market actors: they rationally seek to maximize their 'utility'.
Self-interested bureaucrats and politicians are effectively entrepreneurs who compete to gain control of a monopoly, the state.[14]

But, rather as with MFT, no *empirical* evidence was advanced to support this idea. It was just assumed that social, constitutional and ethical concerns never motivated bureaucrats and politicians. And it was assumed that the public and private sectors were competitors and one side or the other could be a loser.

That is why, if government dares to do anything ambitious, it risks being accused of crowding out private investment. Government investment in a sector, say aircraft-building as with Airbus, the European aerospace company, is assumed to be likely to rob the private sector of profitable opportunities. But the charge assumes a static view of investment possibilities – that there are only a given number of possibilities at any one time – as well as that the public and private sectors are competitors rather than partners. Lurking deeper is the familiar conviction that only the private sector creates value and – by extension – that government investment may destroy it.

In reality, the whole idea of governments crowding out the private sector is usually false. Government investment often has the opposite effect. When structured strategically it can crowd in private investment, stimulating funding that might not have happened otherwise and expanding national output, which benefits public and private investors alike. Public investment in Apollo inspired rapid advances in computing and digital technology through contracts with the private sector. Relatively small government stakes in Airbus have helped build the world's biggest aircraft company, with operations and suppliers across Europe. The history of technological breakthroughs shows that public investment, particularly when made early in the innovation process, absorbs major uncertainties and long-term risks that private investors can be reluctant to take on. Indeed, public investment in the early, high-risk stage of areas like nanotechnology, biotechnology and green technology were critical to the later proliferation of small start-ups, some of which later scaled up. An alternative theory must thus be based on market shaping and market co-creation, a concept we return to in Chapter 6.

Myth 3: Government needs to run like a business

The conviction that government should simply administer without risk-taking runs deep. We're told that government should not transgress beyond ensuring a level playing field in the economy (such as by preventing monopolies), maintaining law and order and regulating where necessary (for example in food safety). The assumption is that not only should the public sector emulate private-sector disciplines, but it ought also to slough off significant slices of activity traditionally held in the public domain to the private sector, such as public transport and public health. This is to avoid the sort of failures that public choice theorists believe they had identified, for example swollen bureaucracies inefficiently running services such as public-health laboratories or stifling competition by controlling electricity prices.

In business schools, mainly in the USA, public choice theory influenced the development of New Public Management (NPM), which gathered momentum in the 1980s. Several strategies were high on the NPM list. One was to introduce some equivalent of the profit motive into the public sector to improve performance – for instance, efficiency targets. An example of this kind of thinking was UK legislation in 1990 to create an internal market in the National Health

Service, under which the government became a purchaser instead of a provider of health services and external suppliers could bid against NHS ones.

Another strategy has been contracting out, franchising or privatizing government services. The purpose here is to address the principal–agent problem: citizens (the principals) cannot hold public-sector employees (their agents) accountable in the way shareholders can the managers of a corporation – in theory at least. Citizens' main sanction in a democratic society is voting, which is intermittent, might have only an indirect effect on bureaucrats and is a poor substitute for the discipline of the profit motive. Because the latter and accountability are held to be weaker in the public sector than in the private sector, the public sector is likely to be less efficient. And there is the idea – which will be a major theme of this book – that government should limit itself to technical efforts to counter market failure and enhance public-sector efficiency by introducing market discipline.[15]

NPM policies were widely implemented in advanced economies in the 1980s and 1990s, in particular in the UK, New Zealand and Australia.[16] By the mid 1990s, however, concerns were growing about the effectiveness of NPM. Deregulation, shareholder value and new government practices, such as setting up arm's-length agencies and outsourcing, were not always working as well as the theory said they should. For instance, deregulation was encouraging highly risky behaviour, as with the banks; shareholder value was enriching executives at the expense of long-term investment; and outsourcing was leading to loss of public control over the quality of services and products.

Trying to run public institutions as though they were

businesses has had severe consequences. Hospital patients have discovered they are 'clients'; students and passengers are 'customers'. Static metrics of efficiency have been introduced into evaluation exercises. These involve value-for-money calculations and cost–benefit analysis (CBA), concerned with allocative or distributive efficiency which parallels economic production to satisfy consumer preferences with the most efficient combination of resources.

CBA involves making the best use of fixed resources at a fixed point in time, calculated by using existing market prices. Yet ambitious projects such as going to the moon or setting up the welfare state involved fundamental uncertainty and feedback loops across many different sectors. Feedback loops occur when a system's output amplifies the system (positive feedback) or hinders the system (negative feedback). Fundamental uncertainty and feedback loops are hard to capture with static metrics such as CBA. One example is the enormous difficulty UK governments have experienced in reliably estimating the cost of offshore wind-generated electricity as little as six months in advance, let alone the twenty-five years which would be a typical planning horizon for energy ventures of this sort. In general, cost estimates have tended to be too high, which is a major failing when set against the certainty of climate change and the pressing need to de-carbonize energy production as much as possible.

Myth 4: Outsourcing saves taxpayer money and lowers risk

Starting in the 1970s, the key idea of NPM – that government's attempts to make things better for people could actually make them worse – firmly gripped politicians, businesspeople and bureaucrats themselves, first in the USA and later elsewhere. Many citizens, whether defined as consumers or users, came to regard government as inefficient and state-owned enterprises as a prime example of government's shortcomings. The impetus was to try to make the public sector as 'efficient' as the private sector. Hence NPM led to proposals to a) privatize publicly owned companies; b) decentralize and/or break up big public organizations; and c) introduce metrics such as performance pay. One way to reduce the risk of government 'doing harm' was to outsource and privatize public services. In theory, outsourcing and privatization would ameliorate the principal–agent problem in the relationship between government and citizens, save money and improve services. The practice turned out to be quite different.

The theory took strong hold, especially in the UK from Prime Minister Margaret Thatcher's first Conservative government in 1979 through to the 1990s and 2000s under New Labour. Its practice took three forms: privatization, public–private ventures and outsourcing. Paradoxically, what was presented as a market-oriented strategy was accompanied by centralization of the state machine, for example by weakening the powers of local government over housing. Many state-owned enterprises in gas, electricity, water, railways, telecommunications and so on were privatized – sometimes with perverse results. While domestic nationalized industries were being abolished, ironically it seemed acceptable that *foreign* nationalized industries could take over running the same enterprises: today, Électricité de France (EDF) supplies gas and electricity in the UK; MTR, majority-owned by the government of Hong Kong and operator of the Hong Kong metro, is part of a consortium which runs Crossrail, London's huge underground railway development; Abellio, wholly owned by the Dutch national rail operator, runs bus and rail services around the UK.

Between 1980 and 1996 the UK accounted for 40 per cent of the total value of all assets privatized across the OECD.[17] Encouraged by multilateral institutions such as the World Bank and International Monetary Fund (the 'Washington consensus'), developing countries also privatized their state-owned enterprises. At the same time, the Private Finance Initiative (PFI) favoured by New Labour sought to establish government partnerships with private companies to build and run public assets such as hospitals, schools, prisons and defence facilities.

NPM naturally argued for smaller government and conventional management of the public finances including, in some versions of the theory, a balanced budget. The government ought to spend no more than its revenues over a given budgetary period, avoid borrowing that increased the national debt and preferably reduce the national debt. This was the underlying ideology of Thatcherism, if not always its practice. After eighteen years out of office, New Labour was anxious not to frighten the fiscal horses and risk being accused of financial irresponsibility. Instead of borrowing at the cheap rates government could command to upgrade hospitals, schools, roads and so on, New Labour adopted PFI so that private companies would finance these undertakings and the government would repay them over the coming years.

In total, there have been over 700 projects financed through PFI in the UK since 1998, with a capital value of around £60 billion. Under the current payment arrangements, these will cost the public purse a cumulative total of nearly £310 billion by 2047–8 – more than five times the original capital outlay. The UK's National Audit Office estimates that the cost of a PFI project is typically around 40 per cent higher than an identical project financed by government borrowing.[18]

Many public services were also outsourced. While PFI was largely about building and running infrastructure, outsourcing was mainly about handing services over to the private sector to manage, notably IT. HMRC (Her Majesty's Revenue and Customs), DVLA (the Driver and Vehicle Licensing Agency), the NHS and local authorities awarded enormous IT contracts to external suppliers. Public services, including rubbish collection, school meals, building maintenance, prisons and even ambulance and probation services, were placed in the hands of private providers, often by local authorities: at its peak in 2012–13, the value of outsourcing contracts awarded by the latter reached £708 million.[19]

Since then, however, the value of local-government outsourced contracts has steadily fallen. The trend is similar for central-government IT outsourcing. Public organizations have increasingly found that outsourcing has not delivered the quality and reliability of services they had expected and has often not been good value for money either. In 2011, for example, the UK government basically gave up on an IT system for patient records in the National Health Service after spending almost £10 billion on it. The causes of the failure were complex, but a decade after the project's inception in 2002 the private contractor had still not delivered the software. A member of the House of Commons Public Accounts Committee, which reported on the saga, described it as 'one of the worst and most expensive contracting fiascos in the history of the public sector'.[20] In 2016, the DVLA ended two decades of outsourcing its IT, took it back in house and trained its staff, who built a new online application in just seven weeks.

The spectacular collapse in 2018 of Carillion, one of the UK's biggest suppliers of outsourced services to government, showed how exposed the government had become to private-sector failure. It also underlined the flaw in NPM theory that assumed public-sector failures were likely to be more serious than private-sector ones. It was the biggest corporate fiasco the Official Receiver (a civil servant and an officer of the court who helps to administer insolvencies) had ever dealt with. Carillion collapsed under the weight of a £7 billion debt mountain, compared with its annual sales of £5.2 billion. According to a report by the Institute for Government, a British think tank, more than 2,000 people (out of a workforce of 18,000) were made redundant and 30,000 suppliers, subcontractors and short-term creditors were owed £2 billion – illustrating how hard it is for government to hold private contractors accountable when supply chains are so long.[21] Another 75,000 people in the supply chain were affected and 450 projects were disrupted, including building hospitals and railways, providing school meals and maintaining prisons and homes for the armed services, often leading to long delays in completion and higher costs.[22]

A report by the National Audit Office found that the collapse had put back the completion of the Royal Liverpool University Hospital, a PFI project, until at least 2022, five years behind schedule, and would cost more than £1 billion to build and run compared with the original estimate of £746 million, partly because of serious construction faults under Carillion. The Department of Health and Social Care paid

£42 million to end contracts with PFI investors in the project. Another major PFI project, the Midland Metropolitan Hospital in Birmingham, was due to open in 2022, four years late, at a cost of £988 million, some £300 million over budget.[23]

Carillion's failure led to accusations by BlackRock, the giant fund manager that was one of the company's investors, that the company thought about 'how to remunerate executives rather than actually what was going on in the business'.[24] The Institute for Government said the government had created a 'corporate monster' with 'low-margin, high-risk' projects – an endemic weakness of the outsourcing model of procurement, particularly for long-term contracts, where contractors are tempted to underbid to increase market share and hope they can increase their margins as the project progresses. It accepted that the government had tried to improve training for civil servants and reformed outsourcing procedures, but said that many departments were still not following best practices and the government was signing risky projects which could collapse in the future, a reference both to Carillion's undercharging and pressure on civil servants to award contracts to the lowest bidder. A combination of weakened public-sector capacity and private-sector ineptitude partly caused by managerial capture of the company (an outcome advocates of shareholder value did not anticipate) had proved disastrous.

In the 1990s and early 2000s, the USA also went in for outsourcing in a big way. In 2006–8 there were nearly four times as many federal contract workers as federal employees (7.6 million compared with 2 million). But by 2015 the ratio had fallen to 2:1, with 3.7 million federal contract workers compared with 2 million federal employees.

The federal government spent an estimated $300 billion on

private contractors in 2003–4 and $500 billion in 2012.[25] In 2017, a Government Accountability Office report stated that federal contractor expenditures were $438 billion for the fiscal year 2015 – nearly 40 per cent of the government's discretionary spending. In civilian agencies, a whopping 80 per cent of contractor expenditures were for services. The largest category was for 'professional supported services', and the report noted that 'contractors performing these types of services are at a heightened risk of performing inherently governmental work.'[26] Translation: work that should largely belong to government workers is going to contractors – as it has in the UK.

Since NPM is supposed to be about efficiency, you would hope that this at least saved the taxpayer money. It seems not. A study by the Project on Government Oversight, an independent watchdog in the USA, shows that the federal government approves service-contract billing rates – deemed fair and reasonable – that pay contractors 1.83 times *more* than the government pays federal employees in total compensation, and more than twice the total compensation paid in the private sector for comparable services.

One study found that, in the UK, reported public administration costs had risen by 40 per cent in real terms between 1985 and 2015. Over the same period, the civil service was cut by a third and public spending doubled. Outsourced operations saw their costs rise the fastest. The numbers of service failures, complaints and judicial challenges also rocketed.[27] Similar problems afflicted privatized industries too and would not surprise, for example, many UK rail travellers. It is true that British Rail, the old state-owned undertaking, was a byword for poor service (though not always for poor engineering). But a quarter of a century after a complex public–private arrangement replaced full state ownership of the railways, fares have tended to rise faster than wages and inflation, the fare structure is complicated and poor service such as unpunctuality frustrates passengers.[28] In the year to June 2019, only 64.7 per cent of trains arrived at their stations on time.[29] Meanwhile, the amount of public subsidy to the sector has more than doubled since privatization, meaning that the profits made by the private operators are ultimately underwritten by the taxpayer.[30] In March 2020, as passenger numbers collapsed under the impact of COVID-19, the government temporarily suspended all rail franchises and replaced them with management contracts, effectively renationalizing the railways, at least for the duration of the health crisis.[31] Like US taxpayers, UK rail customers can be forgiven for wondering whether surrendering services to the private sector has brought good value for money.

Big consultancy firms have been among the biggest winners from outsourcing. Although contracts with firms such as McKinsey, one of the best-known names in the consultancy business, involve millions of taxpayers' money, details can be hard to pin down. But there are some tantalizing glimpses. When the UK began to exit the EU, the Big Four consultancy firms (Deloitte, Ernst & Young, KPMG and PwC) saw their profits rise by 20 per cent. Government spending on these companies rose from £77 million to £464 million[32] between 2018 and 2019 – which is ironic, given that Brexit was meant to save the state money. One could argue that this was just to manage the transition or the setting-up of a project, but the trend has been towards an addiction to consulting companies to manage *basic* operations. There have been two reasons for this. One is the erosion of internal capacities, due partly to budget cuts and partly to lower ambition for government's role. The other reason is the fear of failure.

Early in 2020, the *Financial Times* reported:

> According to a National Audit Office report in 2016, the government is spending more on consultants despite them costing twice as much as civil servants. It found a total of 47 temporary staff were on a daily rate of more than £1,000, compared with 30 senior civil servants with comparable pay. Nor is value for money assured. A University of Bristol study published last year concluded that English NHS acute care hospital trusts became less efficient even as they spent more on outside experts. Despite the best efforts of the NAO and other analysts, however, it can be hard to piece together the full picture. Joshua Pritchard, outsourcing and procurement lead at the Reform think tank, says: 'Without greater transparency in government contracting, it is impossible to examine the total amount spent, the additional benefits being delivered, or whether departments have guaranteed value for money in these deals.'[33]

Such concerns have only been amplified by a string of controversies involving top consultancy firms in recent years. Insiders have lambasted McKinsey's recent restructuring of US security agencies, including the CIA and the National Securities Agency, for hampering key decision-making processes and ultimately increasing organizational inefficiencies.[34] McKinsey won its multi-million-dollar contracts without competitive bidding. Ostensibly this was to accelerate project timelines; in reality, it removed from outsourcing procedures the most basic checks for quality control and accountability.

Such 'no-bid' contracts have increased in use over recent years, and alongside poorly drafted contracts and inefficient performance monitoring have entrenched unsatisfactory outcomes.[35] A quantitative analysis of 120 NHS hospital trusts in the UK between 2010 and 2014 found that spending more on management consultants led to a significant rise in *in*efficiencies and was linked to no improvement in patient outcomes.[36] Over the same time period, NHS expenditure on consultants almost doubled from £313 million to £640 million.[37] A UK parliamentary inquiry into the spectacularly failed contract between UK Trade and Investment (a government department to help UK businesses with overseas trade, replaced in 2016 by the Department for International Trade) and PA Consulting, a UK management consultancy, highlighted that the outsourcing firm had taken advantage of the government's lack of expertise in securing good-value deals on behalf of taxpayers – a fact it emphasized was a 'regular cause for concern'.[38]

A telling instance of the reduction of government capability is that in 1970 the public sector employed 47 per cent of architects in the UK, mostly with local authorities. Today it is less than 1 per cent.[39] This partly reflects the sharp fall in the provision of new public housing by local authorities, but it is also consistent with the outsourcing trend across government. An important reason why the UK struggled to provide enough testing during the coronavirus pandemic was that laboratory capacity, including a once extensive and well-resourced network of public laboratories, had been run down over the previous twenty years.[40]

But the recent explosion of outsourcing public-service functions to consultants has also harboured a darker side. At the height of the European refugee crisis in 2015, the German government paid McKinsey over €29 million to develop 'fast-track' migrant processing centres. The streamlined procedure it developed coincided with increased numbers of refugees being assigned to a temporary residency status that denied them key rights, such as that of family reunification. Legal experts have noted that the neglect of human rights considerations within McKinsey's reorganization has triggered thousands of appeals, effectively shifting the backlog from migrant centres to the German courts.[41] That management consultants can be so bluntly deployed in such an intricate area of human rights law demonstrates how far this thinking has encroached into public policy. More worryingly, it suggests that public values are being sacrificed in the name of efficiency.

Experts question whether the advice consultants give really enhances what an organization's staff can do themselves, and whether the money could be better spent on research into medicines and health-care provision. Use of consultants also raises important questions of accountability, especially when one of their projects goes wrong, and conflicts of interest – for example, when a consultant works simultaneously for a global-health client and a client in a sector such as coal, which harms health. Unfortunately, the secrecy surrounding many consultancy contracts makes it hard to answer these questions definitively.[42]

Schemes like PFI and outsourcing involve complex contracts. Economic theories of contract and property rights are clear that the more complicated a product is, the greater the likelihood of asymmetries of information, whereby the seller – say a private provider of prison services – has more information than the buyer, the government.[43] This leads to several difficulties for government. Trying to manage asymmetrical contracts and remedy their intrinsic weaknesses piles extra costs on the buyer. The government cannot give up its legal and political responsibilities to provide certain services, notably law and order and defence, so private providers can cut corners because the government will continue to pay for the service, at least until it can find an alternative way of providing it – a case of 'moral hazard'. And, as we have seen in Carillion's case, there is a risk that poor contracting leads to the problem being dumped back into taxpayers' laps.

Moreover, it is clear that the negative impact of outsourcing and related practices has frequently gone beyond problems with quality, reliability and cost, important as they are. Put simply, privatization and outsourcing can remove tasks from people with long experience of doing them (civil servants) and give them to people whose experience may be much less (private companies). This is a matter of policy, not inherent capability, as the presence of foreign nationalized industries running privatized UK businesses illustrates. The consequence, however, has often been to hollow out government's capacity, run down its skills and expertise and demoralize public servants, who feel they cannot do their jobs as well as they would like to.

But the real tragedy of this addiction to outsourcing to management consultancies is that it only further undermines the internal capacities of the public sector. This consequence was brought into sharp focus as the COVID-19 pandemic unfolded. Rather than focusing on retraining NHS staff and redeploying civil servants to run its test-and-trace system, as Germany did,[44] the UK government outsourced its pandemic response to a patchwork of consultancy firms. In October

2020, news outlets reported that consultants from Boston Consulting Group (BCG) were being paid as much as £6,250 a day to work on the test-and-trace system.[45] At the time of writing, the full scale of pandemic-related spending on management consultants remains unclear, but its implications for public-sector capabilities are unambiguous. As Lord Agnew, Conservative peer and Minister of State at the Cabinet and HM Treasury put it in September 2020, Whitehall has been 'infantilized' by the reliance on consultancy firms. Not only is outsourcing outrageously expensive, but it deprives 'our brightest [civil servants] of opportunities to work on some of the most challenging, fulfilling and crunchy issues'.[46] In other words, their development – and thus the growth of the public sector – is stunted.

The more private providers undertake public activities, the more government accountability is reduced because capabilities have been diminished and it is harder to change poor policy. Risks are not taken, and rewards are not reaped. The result is a self-fulfilling prophecy: the less government does, the less it takes risks and manages, the less capacity it develops and the more boring it is to work for. At the same time, the more attractive it is to work for a private provider or consultancy firm, the more talent is siphoned away from government.

Myth 5: Governments shouldn't pick winners

The first three myths lead to the idea that government should not steer the economy but only facilitate it. This is often expressed as: governments should stick to the basics and not 'pick winners'. Sarah Palin, the Republican vice-presidential candidate in the 2008 US election, once said: 'Our government needs to adopt a pro-market agenda that doesn't pick winners and losers, but it invites competition and it levels the playing field for everyone.'[47] And even in less ideological circles, well-meaning civil servants often begin white papers stating why their strategy is 'not about picking winners'. Yet this is a false problem. Of course policymakers need to make decisions about what forms of support to provide, and hence to pick.

'Picking winners' refers to government efforts to steer the economy and stimulate activity by choosing and often supporting technologies, businesses and sectors it believes are important and will succeed. There can be many reasons for making a particular choice, including seizing a technological lead, diffusing knowledge, creating jobs, raising productivity and incomes, boosting regional development and defence. Industrial policy – an overall strategy to encourage the development and growth of all or part of the economy, often with an emphasis on manufacturing – can be seen as picking winners writ large. Indeed, whenever the government tries to stimulate a technology or a sector to develop, it is in the broad sense picking winners. The real problem is when losers pick the government.

Many of the objectives may be worthwhile, but picking winners has acquired derogatory overtones because of government's alleged inability to choose wisely – even though the private sector may not be good at picking winners either. Government interventions, it is claimed, too often fail and leave the taxpayer to pick up the tab. They prove that risk is the business of the private sector and, perhaps more importantly, that the private sector either attracts less bad publicity when its ventures fail or has a higher tolerance for bad publicity. Advocates of the 'need to not pick winners' point to cases such as Concorde, the Anglo-French supersonic airliner that flew from 1976 to 2003. It was a technological triumph but cost vastly more than forecast to build and never led to a supersonic revolution in commercial air travel. Another case, in the USA, was Solyndra, a solar-power panel start-up that in 2009 received a $535 million guaranteed loan from the US Department of Energy (DoE), only to file for bankruptcy four years later.

And yet the idea that government cannot pick winners is historically inaccurate.[48] In fact, during periods of technological shifts, government can play a critical role in co-ordinating industrial efforts and setting standards that create markets. But they must make the decision to pick a strategy – and tilt the playing field in that direction. We saw this in the 1990s, when the government of South Korea recognized the enormous potential of high-definition (HD) technology. At the time, the electronics industry was undergoing a shift from analogue to digital products, and South Korea was still a mass-producer of analogue TVs. To build the necessary capabilities to shift to HD products, the South Korean government set up a committee dedicated to co-developing HD TV – comprised of three ministries and more than a dozen private firms, universities and government research institutes – which resulted in the creation of a 'grand research consortium'. The consortium, which was led by the Video Industrial R&D Association of Korea, included the Korea Electronics Institute, the Korea Institute of Industrial Technology, Samsung, LG, Hyundai, Daewoo Electronics and other private-sector firms. With $100 million in combined funding from the government and the private sector, it focused on the technology transfer and absorption from the USA and Japan. The government co-ordinated the work of leading companies to develop standards for digital TV emerging from the USA while also encouraging competition between the companies.[49] Meanwhile, Korean companies established research teams and centres in the USA that were close to universities and other research institutes.[50] In October 1993, after the consortium presented the first prototype for digital TV broadcasting and receiving, the Korean government moved to support the second phase of the project – the industrialization and commercialization of a new prototype. Two years later, the consortium started the development and miniaturization of ASIC chips, and many companies competed to scoop the contract for the final commercial product – which was ultimately launched by Samsung in 1998.[51]

Not all strategies of this type succeed, of course; that is part and parcel of trial and error. But sometimes picking winners is confused with state support for troubled industries, for example when the UK government attempted to help the domestic car industry by forming British Leyland in 1968 and shipbuilding by creating Upper Clyde Shipbuilders that same year. Neither company was successful. But picking winners in the sense of backing what are deemed to be the innovations, sectors and businesses of the future is quite different from trying to keep ailing industries and companies alive. And in the narrow sense of selecting a winning business, governments, just like venture capitalists, will win some and lose some. The same year that the US government made the $535 million guaranteed loan to Solyndra, it also made a similar loan of $465 million to Tesla – now a global leader in the electric revolution that is transforming the automotive industry. China is the world's biggest producer of pencils because it set out to develop a competitive industry, not because it started with comparative advantages in technology or the supply of graphite. Chinese state-owned firms invested in technology and labour, and the government provided cheap finance, tariff protection of domestic producers, lax forest management policies to keep wood cheap, and generous export subsidies.[52]

If a government is to act as an investor of first resort and steer an economy towards meeting goals such as a digital revolution or the green transition, *of course* it will need to make bets and pick winners. But it should pick a direction, and within that direction take a wide portfolio approach. In other words, not pick one technology, or a random sector (usually one of those that lobbies hardest), or even a type of firm (SMEs) – but a direction that can foster and catalyse new collaborations across multiple sectors and have as a key spillover the growth of firms that engage with it. In that sense it is not about picking winners, but picking the willing.

Without the government making bets, we would not have the internet or Tesla. However, the manner in which government does so is important. If it puts all of its eggs in one basket, then there is a danger that it picks wrong and loses everything. But if it acts more like a venture capitalist and structures its investments as a portfolio, then this risk is reduced. Indeed, it was because Obama was interested in steering the economy along a green transition that the DoE provided guaranteed loans to Tesla, Solyndra and other green companies. The fact that one of these failed is only normal; as any venture capitalist will confirm, many failures are required before a success arrives. The real problem is the practice of socializing risks and privatizing rewards, which we return to in Chapter 6.[53] The government bailed out the failed company (Solyndra) but got none of the upside for the successful company (Tesla). Moreover, US citizens knew about the government's role in the failure of Solyndra – which was widely described in the media – but not about its role in the success of Tesla, which was marketed as a private-sector success. This only reinforced the narrative that government should not try to pick winners.

It's also worth remembering that valuable lessons can be learned from failures. It has been argued, for example, that the nationalization of British Leyland in 1975 – triggered by the near-bankruptcy of the car manufacturer – prevented the British car industry from collapse and made possible the future development of a flourishing sector. Nationalizing Rolls-Royce in 1971 had a similar result. As a leading aero-engine manufacturer, Rolls-Royce is now at the heart of the UK aerospace industry, which is 'that rare thing, a world-beating advanced manufacturing sector based in Britain'.[54] And returning to Concorde, although it is no longer flying the investment that went into it produced an array of productive spillovers in different sectors: the high air resistance of supersonic flight meant that engineers had to develop novel cooling systems in Concorde's wings and windows, and a new paint that was twice as reflective to avoid overheating.[55] The challenge of making measurements on Concorde's Olympus engines led Sir David McMurtry to invent the touch-trigger probe, revolutionizing the field of co-ordinate measurement and founding Renishaw, one of the UK's best-known engineering firms, in the process.[56] These spillovers do not mean that Concorde was worth the investment, or good value for money, but they should surely be taken into account in any evaluation of that investment. And yet no proper evaluation exists that does so.

Crucially, however, the way in which the debate has been framed is misleading in a much more fundamental sense. Market failure implies that 'pure' private goods or markets can exist independently of public or collective action: value can be created in the private sector irrespective of government. The subtle and insidious effect of this widely held view is to constrain civil servants with an ideology that says they can as easily do harm as good and chip away at their confidence in their ability to create public value. Civil servants are supposed to implement government policy while at the same time speaking truth unto power. But if government is seriously restricted in what it does, and civil servants do not have the freedom to find out what works, they are likely to become cautious and government's ambition will shrink. Ethos and creativity are crushed. A government that lacks imagination will find it more difficult to create public value.

In reality, value emerges from the interaction of the public and private sectors and civil society. Warren Buffett once said – quite rightly – that 'society is responsible for a very significant percentage of what I've earned.'[57] Indeed, the market and the economy itself can be regarded as *outcomes* of the interactions between these sectors. Government policy is not just 'intervention'. It helps to shape markets, as do many other institutions within and between the public and private sectors: regulators, trade unions, business lobby groups and so on. Government action may be a precondition for others to become involved in a changing economic landscape. More than that, government can actively *co-create* value with business and civil society.

Taken together, these five myths might make one believe that the smaller government is, the better. So instead of thinking about how government can help create public value and build the capabilities to do so, most contemporary political debate about government revolves around its size (ill defined, but often measured by government spending as a percentage of GDP) and budgets. It is much less often about skills and non-financial resources such as training, knowledge, networks and access to expertise. These bear no relation to the size of government or any organization, but are closely associated with real efficiency. And government needs capabilities at many levels, from the top of the political tree to the saplings of local government and specialist agencies.

What matters are the investments that government makes internally – being innovative in how it operates – and externally in the economy in areas that drive long-term productivity growth. The countries in Europe that have the highest debt-to-GDP ratios – which in 2019 were Greece, Italy and Portugal – are also the ones that have not made the necessary investments in the economy, such as in R&D, education, innovation agencies and dynamic public financial institutions.[58]

So, NPM encourages government to take up as little space as possible. But, as previously noted, this has led to outsourcing and privatization. Instead of government going to the moon, it's more as if in recent decades it has been taken for a ride.

PART II: A MISSION POSSIBLE

What it takes to achieve our boldest ambitions

4: Lessons from Apollo: A Moonshot Guide to Change

Do governments really operate as economic theory predicates – fixing markets then getting out of the way for the private sector to innovate and create value? Here is an interesting juxtaposition. On the one hand, there is a self-fulfilling prophecy: we get the kind of government organizations we believe are possible. If the training of civil servants makes them think that at best governments can fix problems, and that government failure is even worse than market failure, it is not surprising that we end up with timid public organizations, unwilling to take risks, giving into pressure to be 'business-friendly', and over time reducing their own capacity to create value. On the other hand, there are many examples of government operating quite differently, investing in internal capacity and working in a dynamic, proactive way, providing a directional shift to the economy and society. From US President Franklin Delano Roosevelt's Depression-era New Deal policies to the co-ordination of industrial transformation in World War Two, and the funding today of projects pushing some of the planet's cities in a green direction, there are plenty of examples that could – if unpicked – remind us what it means to bring ambition to the heart of government.

The ambition of government should be to set off catalytic reactions across society, an important part of which would be performing as a better partner to business – helping steer change towards meeting society's challenges, offering clear rewards for businesses willing to help 'make it happen' and stumping up the high-risk early investments that business tends to shy away from. And in taking such risks, government would be recognized as an active investor – not just a lender of last resort – and command public support for sharing in the rewards.

This is not a pie-in-the-sky ambition. It has happened before. The way that government led the Apollo programme could hardly differ more from conventional thinking about the role of government in the economy, which leaves us ill equipped to tackle the greatest challenges of our time. The public sector set itself a goal hitherto hardly contemplated outside the ranks of science-fiction writers, visionaries and a handful of scientists. It did so with a sense of urgency, with a clear and ambitious objective to accomplish the truly extraordinary: putting a man on the moon and bringing him back safely to a firm and very tight deadline. In thinking about the key attributes of the Apollo programme, six stand out: (1) vision infused with a strong sense of purpose; (2) risk-taking and innovation; (3) organizational dynamism; (4) collaboration and spillovers across multiple sectors; (5) long-term horizons and budgeting that focused on outcomes; and (6) a dynamic partnership between the public and private sectors. If they are scaled up and the lessons for policy are learned, these can be the guiding principles for a new type of challenge-led political economy.

This chapter examines the Apollo programme as an example of an extraordinary feat: government stepping outside the market-fixing role and into the market-shaping one. It looks at how, to get to the moon, government had to break out of the conventions limiting its activities (much as the prevailing theories set out in the last chapter confine governments today) and ask what can be learned if we scale up that sort of bold thinking and doing. Chapter 5 then considers how the principles can also be applied to societal challenges, such as those embodied in the UN's SDGs and Green New Deal policies worldwide.

Leadership: vision and purpose

The moon landing was driven by Cold War competition with the USSR: the urge to beat the Russians galvanized one of the most innovative feats in human history. But what made that feat possible and successful was leadership by a government that had a vision, took risks to achieve it, put its money where its mouth was and collaborated widely with organizations willing to help. And the consequence of Kennedy's decision reached far beyond competition with a rival power: it lifted the gaze of humans to glimpse what outcomes they can achieve.

Apollo 11 – the first mission of the Apollo programme to land on the moon – deeply affected society. People around the world invested their hopes and fears in its success, creating a bond and sense of engagement that went far beyond the technology and the project. Children were inspired to dream of becoming astronauts, reinvigorating science, technology, engineering and maths in schools. NASA staff were no different. The story goes that, on a visit to the NASA Space Center in 1962, Kennedy encountered a janitor at work. He asked the man what he was doing. The janitor famously replied: 'Well, Mr President, I'm helping put a man on the moon.'

Kennedy understood the significance of the public

narrative. Innovation and the commercialization of ideas do not happen because you want them to: they happen along the way to solving bigger problems. Apollo was an example of what can be done if the ambition is inspiring and concrete. Kennedy admitted that the budget for the Apollo programme would be huge by the standards of the time. But in his famous speech at Rice University, he argued that the benefits would make it well worth every cent spent:

> The growth of our science and education will be enriched by new knowledge of our universe and environment, by new techniques of learning and mapping and observation, by new tools and computers for industry, medicine, the home as well as the school . . . And finally, the space effort itself, while still in its infancy, has already created a great number of new companies, and tens of thousands of new jobs. Space and related industries are generating new demands in investment and skilled personnel . . . What was once the furthest outpost on the old frontier of the West will be the furthest outpost on the new frontier of science and space.[1]

It was more than an inspirational vision, though that was important. It also set out a purpose.

And yet Apollo was not devoid of controversy. Among some, it roused scepticism and disapproval. On 15 July 1969, Ralph Abernathy, successor to the slain Martin Luther King and head of the Southern Christian Leadership Conference, spoke at a rally at Cape Kennedy in Florida, saying: 'We may go on from this day to Mars and to Jupiter and even to the heavens beyond, but as long as racism, poverty and hunger and war prevail on the earth, we as a civilized nation have failed.'[2] Shortly thereafter the blues singer Gil Scott-Heron released the track 'Whitey on the Moon', a poetic expression of the persistence of racial inequality in America in the midst of the nation's fixation on a technological feat. He wrote:

A rat done bit my sister Nell.
(with Whitey on the moon)
Her face and arms began to swell.
(and Whitey's on the moon)
I can't pay no doctor bill.
(but Whitey's on the moon)
Ten years from now I'll be paying still.
(while Whitey's on the moon)

Vision and purpose cannot be forced. They require charisma on the part of leaders, but also real engagement with society – both through the media but also through genuine debate. The fact that John F. Kennedy and Martin Luther King were shot dead in the same decade tells us a lot about what charismatic leadership faced in the USA in the 1960s. And modern-day missions that involve social, behavioural and political factors – such as those related to battling climate change – need much more dynamic citizen engagement than purely technological ones do. They do, of course, require vision and inspiration as bold as that of the moon landing – but also much more engagement with citizens in terms of 'who' defines the mission in the first place, and how it is achieved.

Indeed, it is critical to remember that the Apollo project was an intrinsic part of the Cold War. It is because the population of the West saw its security as being dependent on advanced weapons that going to the moon could be a justified way of using an enormous amount of public money. Missions related to global warming will be justified if the environmental-protection direction is socially accepted. Directions must be part of a social consensus, which then justifies both the policies and the missions.

Innovation: risk-taking and experimentation

The Apollo programme was one of the riskiest public-sector projects of the last 100 years and it involved a great deal of experimentation. When Kennedy made his speech, NASA had little except the F-1 engine originally designed by Rocketdyne, a US Air Force contractor, for heavy-payload reconnaissance satellites. The giant Saturn V rocket was under development; computer power was meagre. Above all, there was not even a plan for how to get to the moon. So NASA had to move quickly to find the best way to get there and back.

It considered three options: (1) direct ascent, whereby a single colossal rocket would take astronauts to the moon, land there and bring them back, much as depicted by science-fiction writers and movies; (2) earth-orbit rendezvous, involving two rockets which would meet and dock in earth's orbit, assemble a lunar vehicle from components the rockets had carried and fly that vehicle directly to the moon; and (3) lunar-orbit rendezvous (LOR), whereby a single rocket would take into space three vehicles – a command module, a service module (carrying fuel) and a lunar landing module.[3] LOR specifically referred to the lunar landing module detaching from the command and service modules to take astronauts to the moon's surface and then rejoin those modules, which had been orbiting the moon and would return the astronauts to earth. Eventually, after much debate, the last option was chosen as the most workable solution, even if it was still untried and fraught with risk. It was not just brave. It was probably the single most important decision behind the mission's eventual success.

The extent of the risks was tragically brought home by the Apollo 1 disaster in 1967. Three astronauts – Roger Chaffee, Gus Grissom and Ed White – died during a dry run in the cabin of the command and service module (CSM), the mothership that was to carry them through space, orbit the moon and then bring them back again. The Saturn V rocket was not fuelled, so the risk of a fire was thought to be small. But an electrical spark from damaged wiring caused the pure oxygen and nylon material in the cabin on the top of the rocket to catch fire. There were also technical problems with leakage of coolant, failures in the life support system and glitches with the radios. Internal pressure prevented the hatch door from being opened and the three astronauts in the module were burnt alive.

To carry out the Apollo mission, hundreds of complex problems had to be solved. Some solutions worked, many failed. All came out of a close partnership between government and business: a partnership with a purpose. It required an immense advancement in rocket power. Innovation was also needed in relatively new sectors such as electronics, navigation propulsion, life support, communications and flight controller systems, and in older sectors like textiles, materials and nutrition. But far from fearing failure, experimentation and exploration were welcomed and stimulated through the use of government tools and levers such as goal-oriented procurement policy.

Mission-oriented innovation involves both basic research and the combining of existing technologies into new forms to achieve a task. This, together with active project management and ambitious timescales, accelerated innovation for the Apollo programme. The mission itself could not have worked without a bedrock of invention that pre-existed and had derived from curiosity-driven or blue-skies science. Policies themselves were innovative, often providing no-strings-attached funding to technical groups at various NASA Centers and outside R&D contractors, along with broad guidance for what they needed to produce. This allowed significant free-thinking and innovative solutions to emerge, in contrast to a heavy-handed, central authority dictating solutions to technical teams.[4] In other words, there was a strong underlying innovation system.

There were heart-stopping moments during the Apollo 11 mission too. The men and women in the mission control centre were young, well educated, brave and worked night and day. They guided Neil Armstrong, the mission's commander and the first man to walk on the moon, and Buzz Aldrin in their lunar excursion module (LEM), *Eagle*, which carried the astronauts from the CSM to the lunar surface and back again. Communication loops from the mission control room produced several commands at once because of the need for constant accurate readings. What do the data say? The young staff had to make decisions on the hoof. Solving complex problems was continuous.

When guiding Armstrong and Aldrin during their

descent in *Eagle*, the mission control team always had a binary choice: *land* or *abort*. If things went wrong, the involuntary and dreadful outcome was *crash*. The decisive – possibly fatal – choice was a simple one, but it stemmed from thousands of data points. And the data could produce high drama. The infamous P64 error came at a critical point during the descent to the moon's surface when *Eagle*'s computer flashed up in red the unanticipated error code 1202. John Garman, a twenty-three-year-old engineer, identified the code from a handwritten list he had compiled as indicating that the onboard computer was overloaded. It did not suggest that *Eagle* was off course. Within twenty-seven seconds the chain of command decided: 'We're GO on that alarm.'[5] *Eagle* landed safely.

A valuable lesson from Apollo and other missions is the importance of taking risks and adapting to new information and circumstances. As innovation occurs through trial and error, fear of failure inhibits innovation and learning. Robert H. Goddard, the father of modern rocketry, experimented for years before enjoying any success. Even then, all his rockets failed in modern terms, reaching a maximum height of only 1.6 miles. Goddard was spending relatively small amounts of money, but he could have given up. Instead he saw each 'failure' as a success on the road to his mission of demonstrating that rockets could work.

The average age in the mission control room was twenty-six. The appeal of working for a government agency was that it was not only purpose-driven but also explicitly welcomed risk-taking in the process. Far from being a boring bureaucracy, NASA was the most exciting possible place to be!

Organizational change: agility and flexibility

Risk-taking can be fostered or stunted inside organizations. We have become accustomed to the idea that bureaucracies are slow. But the real question is not whether a bureaucracy should exist or not, but how to turn it into a dynamic organization fuelled by creativity and experimentation. NASA, like many large organizations, was plagued by red tape and poor communication between departments. Wernher von Braun, the Director of the Marshall Space Flight Center, famously said: 'We can lick gravity, but sometimes the paperwork is overwhelming.' The success of NASA in the end was down to its ability over time to develop a more nimble bureaucratic structure, with the agency's top officials announcing goals, but then delegating the hard work and risk-taking to programme offices and centres – top-down management with decentralized project execution and risk-taking.[6] But it took time to build that up.

On the fateful day in 1967, preparing for a test launch of Apollo 1, Gus Grissom was getting frustrated with the lack of communication between different parts of NASA. The bad communication between the ground and spacecraft meant he and his fellow astronauts could not understand what was being said – even though they were both just 100 meters from the control centre on the launch pad. He exasperatedly cried, 'Jesus Christ – how are we going to get to the moon if we can't talk between two or three buildings?!' A couple of hours later he, Chaffee and White were dead.

The faults that that were found to have caused the fire on Apollo 1 were the result not only of poor communication

between different parts and departments of the space programme but also technical problems, as we have seen. Getting
to the moon would require a complete management and
organizational overhaul that allowed more direct communication and collaboration between the astronauts, the designers,
the engineers and mission control. Never was there a greater
need to battle departmental silos.

In 1963, George Mueller, a hard-driving electrical engineer, arrived at NASA from Bell Labs to head NASA's Office
of Manned Space Flight, a post he held until 1969. He found
that NASA, two years into a ten-year mission, was divided
into silos and communications were poor. Buildings and
departments of the rapidly growing organization were not talking to each other. The number of people involved in the
Mercury (1958–63) and Gemini (1962–6) programmes – the
programmes putting astronauts into earth's orbit – stood at
300 or 400, an entirely manageable number. In reality, over
300,000 people were involved in Apollo (1960–72) at its
height, drawn mainly from 20,000 contractors and 200 universities in eighty countries as well as from NASA itself. This
posed an enormous management challenge for NASA.

An example of the scale of the challenge was the development of the CSM. NASA had given clear specifications for
the module to a company then called North American Avi-
ation, which was to build it; this was its first spacecraft. In
1964 George Abbey, a systems engineer for NASA, visited
North American to check on progress. He discovered chaos.
The head of North American knew little about the project.
North American's engineering groups and planning were not
well co-ordinated and were becoming increasingly over-
whelmed by time pressures. The team in charge were angry

because for months they had been unable to reach agreement with NASA on their design for the module. Similar problems afflicted the development of the Saturn V's second stage, for which North American were the contractors as well.

Mueller and others believed that the poor communications were NASA's worst managerial bottleneck. He set about with determination to remedy the problem and in the process transformed the organization. Mueller was a powerful advocate of 'systems management', which he defined as: 'a structure for visualizing all the factors involved as an integrated whole, much as system engineering visualizes all of the physical aspects of a problem'. It is really, he said, system engineering applied to management and permits the system manager to 'recognize the nature and interaction of complex procedures in advance of their becoming problems'. System engineering, whose origins date back to the early twentieth century, had been applied in America to projects such as building the Minuteman intercontinental ballistic missile. The concept can be defined as seeing the design of the whole rather than that of the parts. It is by nature interdisciplinary – a vital quality for NASA. 'It requires you to really understand all of the forces that are brought to bear on a particular system and you've got to take account of "whatever" or else the system won't work the way it's supposed to,' Mueller said.[7]

The aim was to manage the project with an overall understanding of the whole system so that all the complex elements were properly integrated. Many of NASA's problems came from the failure of integration and the puzzle of how to make sure the elements of the programme – not least the physical hardware such as the parts – fitted together technically and on schedule for when they were needed. Integrating the system required connecting disparate teams and specialities (contractors, scientists, engineers, military officers, managers) and creating an organization-wide understanding of the whole.

To achieve this, the entire management system was overhauled, including planning, documentation, inspection and testing to co-ordinate the efforts of very large interdisciplinary teams. Mueller introduced a new management function whose principal purpose was radically to improve communications within NASA. He launched a 'matrix management' system under which the heads of NASA's five centres (programme control, systems engineering, testing, reliability and flight operations) reported directly to him and teams in the centres reported both to Mueller and to their direct superiors. Different teams in different centres were required to communicate with their counterparts at other centres and on other teams. The result of this 'five-box' structure was that the five HQ teams had similar structures and were encouraged to have strong interdepartmental communication. A single individual was clearly responsible for each key area, and for communicating the knowledge acquired. In the end, NASA was able to combine centralized planning and control with decentralized project execution.

Mueller extended the principle to NASA's contractors. They were encouraged to work on site at NASA so they could get an overview of the whole project. There were regular meetings between NASA and the CEOs of contractors, and between NASA experts and their counterparts within the contractors. He cultivated personal contacts with the CEOs, visited their plants and sometimes made speeches there. He tried to drill down to a level where he could personally call CEOs and ask what had happened to a particular piece of equipment. At the same time, Mueller rewrote NASA's contracts with suppliers so they were incentivized to meet schedules – essential if Kennedy's ambition was to be realized. Rewriting the contracts also concentrated the minds of NASA engineers on what they really needed. In addition, Mueller broke chunks of the whole project down into smaller packages, each led by its own manager, such as communications between astronauts and mission control, or the design of the LEM itself. This more dynamic set-up was so successful that businesses copied it: Boeing took up the idea to develop the 747, which also first flew in 1969.

Although there was a clear chain of command, communications became both more horizontal and more vertical. Information flowed across projects and up and down management. The mindset that emerged embraced the readiness and the need to solve complex problems with many unknowns, often quickly and under pressure. Simulation and experimentation led to continuous learning by doing. Communications between functions became dynamic: they adjusted to changing circumstances. The entire organization was able to communicate far more effectively than in traditional organizations working in silos, as had been the case with NASA, so that 'all of us understand what was going on throughout the program . . . [C]ommunications on a level that is free and easy and not constrained by the fact that you're the boss . . . [This was] the secret of the success of the program, because so many programs fail because everybody doesn't know what it is they are supposed to do,' Mueller said.[8]

Mueller's reforms were undoubtedly instrumental in the triumph of the Apollo programme. Still, it was not all plain sailing. Astronauts who had undertaken earlier tests in the

CSM complained privately that there were serious problems with the design and workmanship. In the first years of the crewed space programme from 1961 to 1967, NASA had flown numerous successful flights and poured enormous resources into the Mercury and Gemini programmes. But it had devoted so much of its attention to these first crewed flights that the design and construction of the vehicles that would take men to the moon had been neglected. The Apollo 1 disaster tragically confirmed astronauts' fears and put the whole programme at risk.

Astronauts and test pilots alike accepted that catastrophe during a mission was a possibility, but to lose people on the ground during a launch rehearsal test was an indictment of the whole programme. Quick learning was essential. Gene Kranz, NASA's (second) Chief Flight Director for both Gemini and Apollo, concluded after the Apollo 1 fire that important problems were still not being addressed decisively, despite Mueller's efforts. In a hard-hitting speech to his staff after the disaster he delivered a rallying cry, spelling out with direct honesty what it meant to deliver competence. His main message was that each individual had to take responsibility for the different systems and procedures that hadn't worked. Space flight was fraught with danger, and nothing less than total commitment to the best they could do was acceptable. But there was another message, too. People were not saying, 'This isn't right. Let's shut it down.' Kranz had each member of the control team write at the top of the blackboards in their offices: 'Tough and competent'. The slogan was not to be removed until NASA had put a man on the moon.[9] Just like mechanical systems, management systems need constant maintenance.

After a detailed inquiry lasting six months, the module was redesigned. The next twenty-one months saw a burst of renewed vigour and energy. Apollo 2 was cancelled, and other test flights were rescheduled as NASA sought to verify that the improvements were working. In October 1968 Apollo 7 flew for the first time, with the redesigned command module and near-complete success. A little more than a month later, NASA made its boldest decision yet and launched Apollo 8, the first crewed mission to leave earth's gravity. NASA was back on schedule.

How NASA grappled with crises, as well as reforming its management, shows that solutions are found by organizations and people willing to participate and experiment, not by picking supposedly good solutions in advance and trying to make them work. Experimenting with a portfolio of different solutions to a problem can be likened to classic insurance policy: it avoids putting all the eggs in one basket, which is the danger with alighting on a single solution too early.

The role of top management is to identify essential data and make sure it reaches the right people; it's also to be constantly refocusing on the problem in a process of communication where information flows freely up and down the hierarchy and across departments. Staff in implementing agencies can consolidate project results from the portfolio to see what works best. Missions therefore need the freedom to say how resources are allocated within and between projects and to decide on progress milestones and technical goals during a project's life.

Running a mission-oriented system of innovation requires leadership that – like NASA – encourages risk-taking and adaptation and can attract the best talent. It is important that agencies carrying out missions have sufficient autonomy to take risks without their authority being questioned. Autonomy also makes room for the organizational flexibility necessary for a mission-oriented body to respond quickly to changing conditions and the development of novel technologies. Allowing autonomy in pay helps agencies to recruit top talent with the skills to manage complex networked missions. With this combination of autonomy, flexibility and support from high levels in government, implementing agencies can empower their staff to embrace the inherent risk and push forward the projects that emerge to carry out the mission, while turning off the funding tap for those that turn out to be less promising.

Risk-taking and learning in government require working outside of the usual silos, co-ordinating across policy fields and finding the synergies that turn the components of co-operation into a whole that is larger than the sum of its parts. A mission can easily span ministries, departments, regional and local government bodies. But the greater the need for organizational transformation, the harder it is to accomplish. This is the 'complexity paradox' of modern public policy: the more complex policy issues are, the more compartmentalized policymaking becomes, fragmented into different and sometimes competing government departments and initiatives.[10] On top of that, complex organizational structures with rigid, formal processes can limit the flow of information, reduce openness and constrain creativity. Breaking down silos means setting up a more horizontal relationship between departments, as Mueller did. A mission to tackle air pollution, for example, would need to work across all relevant departments, such as energy, environment, transport, health and finance. Each department retains clear responsibility for its contribution, but the synergies arise from co-ordination from the top of government, while stimulating the innovation from below, as described above. Organizational innovation is both a necessary propellant of missions and a result of them.[11]

NASA's decentralization, with delegation of authority to laboratories such as the Jet Propulsion Laboratory (JPL) in Pasadena California (part of Caltech), was key to its success. So was its ability to sidestep the usual bureaucratic procedures. As discussed by Arnold Levine in his study of management inside NASA, vital for its dynamism and speed was the ability to 'negotiate contracts up to a specified amount, to transfer funds between programs, to start new research tasks without seeking specific authorization, to shift manpower from one division to another, and so on. The strategy of senior management was to give the centers what they needed to get the job done but not so much that their work would lose its relevance to the agency's mission.'[12] Furthermore, dynamic procurement and HR practices allowed NASA to attract talent and contract to the most innovative firms. As Levine further writes:

> Another element in the success of the NASA organization was flexibility: flexibility for the Administrator to appoint to excepted positions, to award major R&D contracts without competitive bidding, to reprogram within appropriation accounts and to transfer between them, to devise and administer a custom-tailored entrance examination, and the like. Examples such as these represent flexibility within the system, not a departure from it; variances from the norm were allowed by Congress, the Bureau of the Budget, and the Civil Service Commission.

This flexibility allowed for that 'free play of the joints' without which institutional rigor mortis sets in. The use of excepted positions, for example, served not only to retain employees within the organization but also to bring in new blood and to expose NASA to outside influences.[13]

In 1958, the same year as NASA was founded, the US government also set up DARPA, the innovation agency of the US Department of Defense – most noted for its investment in what became ARPANET, today's internet. Both were results of Cold War investments. And, similarly to NASA, DARPA's key characteristics are its organizational flexibility, which includes independence from government, flat internal structures, hiring outside of standard government processes, and flexible contracts.[14] The organization encourages bottom-up design, which means that design is left to people like programme managers. They allow discretion in project choice and offer active project management. And indeed, without DARPA there would be no internet to have fuelled the twenty-first-century innovations. Better understanding the organizational structures that have encouraged problem-solving, risk-taking and horizontal collaborations is thus key to understanding the wave of future radical change.

Spillovers: serendipity and collaboration

The successes of organizations that take risks and are directed at large goals are often unpredictable. Innovation itself is often characterized by unpredictable spillovers: the search for one thing leads to the discovery of another – unexpected technological benefits from R&D that can also produce wider managerial, social and economic benefits. Viagra, for example, was initially intended to treat heart problems and then was found to have another application. Innovation is fuelled best when serendipity is allowed, so that multiple paths are pursued, bringing advances in unknown areas. Embracing that uncertainty and serendipity is key for any entrepreneurial organization, whether in the public or private sphere. And as the story below illustrates, such serendipity in technological innovation can also bring great societal benefits.

In 1970, a Zambia-based nun, Sister Mary Jucunda, echoed Ralph Abernathy's concerns in a letter she wrote to the scientific director of NASA, Ernst Stuhlinger.[15] Jucunda asked Stuhlinger how he could justify the use of resources to go to Mars – the next mission after the moonshot – when there was so much suffering on earth: sick children, hunger and inequality. Indeed, this was the same question that Martin Luther King asked while testifying, on issues related to race and urban poverty, to the US Senate in 1966. King observed: 'In a few years we can be assured that we will set a man on the moon and with an adequate telescope he will be able to see the slums on earth with their intensified congestion, decay and turbulence. On what scale of values is this a program of progress?'[16]

Stuhlinger's answer to the nun's question came with a combination of gentleness, conviction and clarity. He first acknowledged what he called her 'depth of a searching mind and compassionate heart'. He admitted the space budget was big and that there were dire needs on earth that also deserved having money spent on them. And yet the space budget was only a third of 1 per cent of US GDP, and only 1.6 per cent of total government expenditure. Still, large it was, and on that basis should still be questioned. He enclosed the famous photograph of 'Earthrise' taken by the astronaut William Anders from Apollo 8 as it orbited the moon on Christmas Eve 1968.[17]

Stuhlinger asked the nun first to consider the story of a benign and much-loved count who lived in Germany 400 years ago.[18] The count was always distributing his riches to the poor. But he did more than redistribute; he created. The count funded the scientific activities of a strange local man who worked in a small laboratory grinding lenses from glass, and then mounting the lenses in tubes and creating small gadgets. The count was criticized for wasting money on the craftsman when the needs of the hungry were so much greater. And yet, explained Stuhlinger, it was precisely such experiments that later paved the way for the invention of the microscope, which proved one of the most useful devices for fighting disease, poverty and hunger: 'The Count, by retaining some of his spending money for research and discovery, contributed far more to the relief of human suffering than he could have contributed by giving all he could possibly spare to his plague-ridden community.'

Stuhlinger then encouraged Sister Jucunda to consider how so many crucial advances that have targeted poverty – advances in nutrition, hygiene, energy and medicine – have resulted from similar scientific studies, whose benefits might initially seem too remote given other immediate urgencies. But scientific progress, he wrote, almost always comes from trying to apply new knowledge to solve problems: 'significant progress in the solutions of technical problems is frequently made not by a direct approach, but by first setting a goal of high challenge which offers a strong motivation for innovative work, which fires the imagination and spurs men to expend their best efforts, and which acts as a catalyst by including chains of other reactions.'

The innovation and risk-taking involved in the entire Apollo programme generated many spillovers. Perhaps one of the greatest was the wave of miniaturization in the computer sector, spurred by the need to get the Apollo guidance computer into a small lunar module. Indeed, the weight and energy consumption of electronics fell exponentially between 1940 and the late 1960s – as recalled by Jean Creighton, a NASA airborne astronomy ambassador, 'from the 30 tons and 160 kilowatts of the Electric Numerical Integrator and Computer to the 70 pounds and 70 watts of the Apollo guidance computer. This weight difference is equivalent to that between a humpback whale and an armadillo.'[19]

Apollo was government-led, and its partnership with business produced numerous important innovations, starting naturally with aerospace. The science and technology underlying Apollo had to shift from a World War Two emphasis on missiles and planes to rockets. Design changed from aerodynamics and comfort to light weight and safety.

Rockets and spacecraft are not enough to get you to the moon. NASA also needed a navigation system to take you there. One of the major hurdles they had to negotiate, and quickly, was how to navigate in outer space. The Polaris missile had a highly developed inertial navigation system. The physics of this were understood, but the application of the navigation technology outside earth's atmosphere posed significant new challenges and would require new systems and hardware.

The navigation system had to work with the two spacecraft needed to reach the surface of the moon: the CSM, the
mothership that was to carry the astronauts through space, orbit
the moon and bring them back again, and the LEM, *Eagle*,
which was to carry astronauts from the CSM in lunar orbit,
land them on the moon and return them to the mothership.

NASA's first major contract in 1961, therefore, was for a
guidance and navigation system. It chose MIT Instrumentation Laboratory, largely because of one man, Charles Draper,
a professor of aeronautical engineering and founder of the
laboratory, who had secured MIT's reputation during World
War Two for precision instrumentation and miniaturization.
The problem was huge. MIT needed not only to come up with
a navigation and guidance system but also with a new kind of
computer which could be installed in the LEM. The system
also had to bring together all the information necessary to
control the two modules.

At that time, such a system was little more than an idea.
Nothing like it had ever been built or tested. Before Apollo,
all aircraft and spacecraft were operated by pulleys and wires
to open and close valves to fly the craft. Astronauts were pilots
used to working a plane's controls manually. But a major concern was that landing on the moon using only manual controls
would use up too much fuel. NASA was also concerned that
the LEM could not bear the weight of a conventional manual
control system. The solution was a computer system that
could control the spacecraft's subsystems, turn valves off and
on, calculate and store data, and so on. It was a tall order. The
technology had to change from hydraulics to electronics.
Adding to the difficulties, computers were then enormous by
modern standards, often required numerous staff to operate

them, and had a poor reputation for reliability. Astronauts were being asked to fly with pre-programmed computers, but were so disenchanted with them that they apparently said that the first thing they would do in space was 'turn the sucker off'. And indeed, Armstrong overrode the computer in last seconds of the lunar landing.

Building the computer depended heavily on two contemporary developments in the electronics industry: the integrated circuit and software writing. Elden C. Hall, who had worked with Draper on Polaris, was given the task of building the hardware. A small computer at the time was the size of a closet. Hall had to squeeze it down to the dimensions of a large shoe box weighing no more than 70 pounds. And he had another major problem. Because many people believed a computer could not be relied upon to fly a spacecraft, Hall knew he not only had to build a small, reliable computer but also convince the sceptics that it could do the job.

Hall took an enormous risk to achieve size and reliability. He chose an emerging technology: integrated circuits, known today as silicon chips. He bought large numbers of them from Fairchild Semiconductor, a Californian company, to test them. Choosing integrated circuits was controversial, but Hall convinced Apollo's programme managers that it was the way forward. At the same time, IBM was developing the Saturn V Instrumentation Unit based on more conventional technology, which included a different guidance computer for the Saturn V. Hall knew that without these integrated circuits there was little chance that a computer with the capacity to do the job could be built in time, and that without it reaching the moon was impossible. At the Apollo programme's peak, MIT was buying 60 per cent of the total output of chips manufactured in the USA. This was an enormous boost to a new technology and to the economies of scale that led to the cost reduction in chips. Additionally, the companies manufacturing them could point to Apollo, a very prestigious project, as an example of their nascent technology's value. Integrated circuits became the basis for the entire US computer industry. In many ways, the Apollo guidance computer can be seen as the world's first portable computer. Indeed, its performance was roughly comparable to late 1970s home computers such as the Commodore PET and Apple II.

Software was another big hurdle to overcome. We take it for granted that even the best computer hardware is only as good as its software. But in the 1960s the word 'software' was still fairly new. In the short contract that NASA signed with MIT, only one line refers to MIT Instrumentation Lab creating the necessary programs. Margaret Hamilton, director of the Software Engineering Division of the MIT Instrumentation Laboratory, led the team developing Apollo's on-board flight software. She introduced more efficient organization into programming, clarifying rules and protocols which became known as 'software engineering'.

To develop the software, NASA called upon the skills of a new breed of scientist responsible for writing thousands of lines of computer code on which Apollo depended to reach its goal. These programmers proved to be some of the most ingenious and creative people in the entire Apollo mission, in part because the programmes required constant corrections. It was the first time that this aspect of computer operations had been given so much importance: this was an essential endeavour, fraught with potential errors, highly complex and expensive, that absolutely had to be carefully thought through. Mistakes could be fatal.

This investment and innovation in electronics and computing resonates today. The development of computing hardware and software for Apollo went on to fuel the IT revolution – and with it the social, political and economic upheavals we are living through. Much of the technology in our smartphones, such as the camera, the telecommunications software and integrated circuits, can trace its origins to the moon landing and related missions.[20]

One unexpected result was to turn product psychology on its head: smaller computers attracted more kudos than bigger ones. Motorola, with a $15.5 million contract from NASA, built the data uplink and digital system, including the technology that allowed listeners and viewers at home to share the nail-biting tension of the landing. The technology became the basis of the telecoms equipment that Motorola still manufactures today.

Apollo's public–private collaboration and experimentation produced innovation in many other sectors such as food, medicine, materials, biology, microbiology, geology and even toilets as well as aerospace engineering, electronics and computing. All this innovation generated many unexpected spin-offs, some physical and some social. NASA's innovations led to CorningWare (glass-ceramic cookware) and Teflon but also new materials with much broader applications, without which the mission would have been impossible. After the Apollo 1 disaster, for example, NASA set out to find a material that would protect astronauts from intense heat and would not catch fire or melt. The solution that was developed is still used in suits for firefighters.

On the social side, the huge increase in computer pro-gramming for Apollo created wholly new jobs, many of which were filled by women. The women programmers were called computers! Many of the 'computers' were African Americans who in NASA's early years worked in a racially segregated unit. Prominent among NASA's female employees was Kath-erine Johnson, an African American mathematician who mastered complex calculations on orbital mechanics, which she was able to make extraordinarily fast. She was a symbol of the changes in American society in the 1960s and her life was the subject of the 2016 film *Hidden Figures*.

Indeed, the most important spillovers are the ones con-cerning people – the people who were trained during the space programme, many of whom later moved from NASA to busi-ness, fuelling the IT sector with some of the most able talent in the country.

Many of these spin-offs could have appeared quite inde-pendently of whether Armstrong had set foot on the moon. But Apollo concentrated minds and effort to force the pace of innovation. At least as important as the spin-offs, however, was the *process* of this massive science- and innovation-led mission. Innovations required researchers from different dis-ciplines and sectors to co-operate to solve problems. While there was a top-down direction (go to the moon and back!), the way different problems were solved was left to individual organizations rather than micromanaged, which would have killed innovation from the start. This open-ended way of framing a problem stimulated new types of risk-taking in

Figure 1 (*following pages*): Twenty things we wouldn't have without space travel

85

20 THINGS
WE WOULDN'T HAVE
WITHOUT SPACE TRAVEL

Camera Phones

In the 1990s a team at the Jet Propulsion Laboratory (JPL) worked to create cameras small enough to fit on spacecraft and with scientific quality. 1/3 of all cameras contain this technology.

Scratch-resistant Lenses

The Lewis Research Centre attempted to develop diamond-hard coatings for aerospace systems, later creating a technique that was developed and patented for just that purpose.

CAT Scans

A space programme needs a good digital image. The JPL played a lead role in developing this technology, which in turn helped create CAT scanners.

LEDs

Red LEDs are being used in space to grow plants and heal humans on earth. LED technology used by NASA has contributed to the development of medical devices such as WARP 10.

Land Mine Removal

Thiokol Propulsion uses NASA surplus rocket fuel to produce a flare that can safely destroy landmines. It works by burning a hole through the mine without detonation.

Athletic Shoes

Nike Air Trainers wouldn't exist if it weren't for suit construction technology developed by NASA. It was a former NASA engineer that first pitched the idea.

Foil Blankets

These metallic sheets, which are now used on earth in extreme temperatures, evolved from a lightweight insulator NASA developed to protect spacecraft and people in space.

Water Purification Systems

In the 1960s, NASA created an electrolytic silver iodizer to purify astronauts' drinking water. This technology is now widely used to kill bacteria in recreational pools.

Dust Busters

NASA approached Black & Decker to develop a lightweight device to collect samples on the moon. The company then used this technology to create the Dustbuster in 1979.

Ear Thermometers

NASA and Diatek developed an 8-ounce aural thermometer, which uses infrared astronomy technology to measure the amount of energy emitted by the ear drum.

Home Insulation

Space is a place of extreme temperatures, knowing this NASA developed insulation from aluminised polyester called Radiant Barrier, used today in most home insulations

The Jaws of Life

An extrication tool to free people from mangled vehicles, the Jaws of Life applies a miniature version of the explosive charge used to separate devices on the space shuttle.

Wireless Headsets

NASA, being one of the forerunners for advancing communication technology, developed these headsets to allow astronauts to be hands-free.

Memory Foam

Memory foam matresses are the result of an incredible foam developed by NASA in the 1970s to help make airline pilots' seats more comfortable. They were later installed in space shuttles.

Freeze-dried Food

NASA conducted extensive research into space food; one technique they developed was freeze drying, which retains 98% of the nutrients and weighs only 20% of the original weight.

Adjustable Smoke Detector

While NASA didn't actually invent the first smoke detector, it did come up with a more modern version, creating the most sophisticated alarm system ever.

Baby Formula

Infant formulas now contain a nutritional enrichment ingredient, the origins of which can be traced back to NASA-sponsored research that explored the use of algae for long-duration space travel.

Artifical Limbs

NASA's innovations into shock-absorption materials, coupled with robotic and extra-vehicular activitie's are being adapted to create more functionally dynamic artificial limbs.

Computer Mouse

In the 1960s a NASA researcher was trying to make computers more interactive when an idea was suggested about how best to manipulate data on a computer screen, leading to the mouse.

Portable Computer

The SPOC was created by adapting the GRiD Compass, the first portable laptop. In its creation hardware had to be modified and new software developed, which propelled the commercial market.

Sector	Spin-off technology
Consumer	Shock-absorbing foam used in athletic shoes Cordless, portable electronics, e.g. vacuum cleaners, drills Quartz precision timepieces Vibration-sensing intruder detectors Freeze-dried food
Industry	Solar panels Liquid methane fuel Earthquake simulators Insulative and fire-resistant materials Hazardous gas detectors Breathing support apparatus Cooling suits Water purification technology
Medicine	Implantable automatic heart defibrillators Computer-programmable pacemakers Kidney dialysis technology Medical imaging, e.g. CAT and MRI scanners

Table 1: Selected technologies enabled by the NASA Apollo programme

many different sub-projects. A lot of these failed, but the failures were part of the mission's overall success. Setting clear goals while allowing bottom-up experimentation stimulated creativity and innovation and produced a winning formula. Missions pick the willing – the organizations across the economy that are prepared to work together.

Finance: outcomes-based budgeting

Missions tend to be long-term, but budgets tend to be short-term and sway with the political winds. NASA's expenditure seemed large at the time and was questioned by politicians and advocacy groups, as we have seen. There is much less doubt today, however, that Apollo was good value for money as well as being an epoch-making mission that stimulated some of the most important innovations in the IT revolution. Indeed, in a press conference in 1964, von Braun told journalists who were asking him about the cost of Apollo that he did not understand why that was a worry. NASA was, according to him, 'creating value and putting more back into the pockets of the Treasury than what was being taken out'.[21] Without using fancy economic jargon, he was basically referring to what economists call the 'multiplier' effect – the overall effect that a dollar of government investment might have in the economy, beyond that dollar. Multipliers occur when one stream of spending and investment spurs another stream (e.g. public investment in the building of a bridge causes an increase in consumption spending by workers making the bridge, and so on). It also comes when there are strong spill-overs between investment areas, such as those discussed above.

In 1961, Kennedy estimated that the first moon landing would cost $7–9 billion[22] ($60–77.2 billion in 2020 dollars), but NASA Administrator James E. Webb encouraged him to double that amount. Webb recognized that the mission could not be launched on the cheap – and, in fact, a meagre budget would set it up for failure. In the end, NASA's budget appropriations from 1960 to 1973 (the year after the last Apollo mission) totalled $56.6 billion ($326.8 billion in 2020 dollars).[23] The Apollo programme cost $25.8 billion, a little less than half of that. Between 1959 and 1972, NASA accounted for about 2.2 per cent of all US federal outlays. Apollo took up about 1.1 per cent of federal outlays over the same period and involved more than 400,000 workers – NASA employees, university researchers and contractors. To put NASA into perspective, total interest payments on the US federal budget debt from 1959 to 1972 were $140.3 billion, and the cost of the Interstate Highway System between 1956 and its official completion in 1991 was $114 billion (equivalent to $214.6 billion in 2020).[24] Given the resources needed, Kennedy called Apollo an 'act of faith and vision'. But he was clear that he thought that achieving the aim, and the spillovers from the endeavour, would be more than worth the budget and the underlying risk, and that 'we must pay what needs to be paid.'[25]

Kennedy was effectively saying that missions should be judged by outcomes, not costs in a normal budgetary sense. Congress did later question the expense, but if Apollo had been evaluated in the way that government finance departments evaluate projects today using CBA, Armstrong and Aldrin would probably never have set foot on the moon – and none of the unforeseen spin-offs would have occurred.

There was certainly a political imperative – to win the space race – and the psychological possibility of boosting national self-confidence and prestige. But Apollo in particular and missions in general ought also to be assessed by their

	Actual	2020 prices
Spacecraft	$8.1 billion	$80 billion
Launch Vehicles	$9.4 billion	$97.3 billion
Development & Operations	$3.1 billion	$28.2 billion
Direct Project Costs	**$20.6 billion**	**$205.3 billion**
Ground Facilities, Salaries & Overheads	$5.2 billion	$53.8 billion
Total Project Apollo	**$25.8 billion**	**$260 billion**
Robotic Lunar Program	$907 million	$10.1 billion
Project Gemini	$1.3 billion	$13.8 billion
Total Lunar Effort	**$28 billion**	**$283 billion**

Table 2: The cost of the Apollo programme 1960–1973

creation of society-wide value, dynamic efficiency over the long term and additional investment generated by stimulating economic activity that would not have occurred otherwise. This is even true, too, of some of the more classic (and narrow) large aeronautics projects such as Concorde: a full assessment of its societal value, for instance, should include the cross-sectoral investments and innovations it stimulated, in jet engine technology, material development, manufacturing techniques and wing shape. The questions to ask about economic and societal missions are: what are we trying to achieve? How will we get there? What kind of markets do we want to create to meet our objectives?

Apollo truly launched the USA into a future of beyond-earth ventures – a future which developed into Skylab, American's first space station, docking in 1975 with the Soviet Soyuz spacecraft, and today the International Space Station, the growth of a 'space economy', commercial ventures in low-earth orbit such as SpaceX, and a return to the moon as a possible jumping-off point for a mission to Mars. At its grandest, Apollo began to open up the realistic possibility that humans may be able to shrug off the limitations of living on earth for ever, and even that as a species we can escape the consequences of the ecological havoc we are wreaking on our own planet. But it also induced a new era of environmental concern, symbolized by the famous 'Earthrise' photograph which contrasted the lifeless desert on the moon with a colourful, living earth. It suggested that development of space technologies can improve life on earth, not escape it – exactly the point made by Stuhlinger.

These are impressive, literally far-reaching outputs. If some seem abstract or idealistic, Figure 2 below puts the

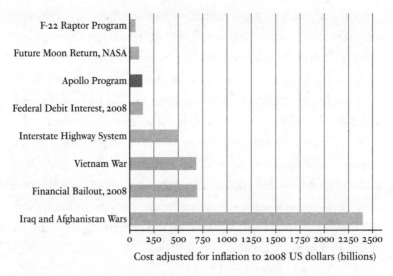

Figure 2: Cost comparison of major US government expenditures

Apollo programme's value for money in sharp perspective.[26] The figures are in 2008 dollars. It is hard to argue that Apollo was a waste of money when set against the colossal costs of wars in Vietnam, Iraq and Afghanistan. It is also worth noting that Apollo cost about a quarter of the $700 billion budgeted for the bankers' bailout in 2008 ($833.6 billion in 2020 dollars), a figure which excludes the wider social and economic costs of the financial crisis.

So, whereas the common budgeting practice is to give departments money to cover inputs irrespective of the goals, outcomes-based budgeting focuses on the outputs. The purpose of the budget is to help fulfil the mission to which it is allocated, whether it be putting a man on the moon or eliminating homelessness or building a carbon-neutral city, an area we explore in the next chapter.

Business and the state: partnership
with a common purpose

During the Apollo mission, NASA did not use consulting companies to do 'project management'. It sought partnership with business and made use of flexible procurement contracts to source to those innovative businesses it thought would deliver. And it wanted that relationship to be direct, not mediated via intermediaries.

The National Aeronautics and Space Act which founded NASA in 1958 allowed it to enter into contracts with 'any person, firm, association, corporation, or educational institution'.[27] This basically gave NASA freedom to work out its contracting procedures, within strict procurement guidelines similar to those used by the armed services but adapted to the needs of NASA, an innovative agency in its infancy. While some funds were set aside to work with small businesses, NASA could work with whatever organization that it thought would get the job done. The 1947 Armed Forces Procurement Act was (often) used, by both the Defense Department and NASA, to waive formal advertising requirements so as to hire the best possible partners in the business community as quickly as possible – even if they might cost more than others. The deciding factors were proven capabilities and experience, not just cost. Indeed, one of the reasons why much business was done with McDonnell-Douglas for rocket-launch vehicles was due to its experience and proven capability to do the kind of work that was needed. Levine argues that going to a new source would have cost NASA an additional $10–20 million and delayed launch schedules by eighteen to thirty months, certainly missing Kennedy's target. As explained by NASA's procurement director, Ernest Brackett:

> ... the nature and scope of the work is such that very special technical, management, and organizational capabilities are required. In such situations, while it cannot be said that there is only one company capable of performing the work, a particular company nevertheless stands out among all others as possessing a superior combination of the requisite, and sometimes unique, skills.[28]

However, it was also recognized that relying excessively on single companies created too much dependency and a weaker bargaining position, so there was a need both to work with reliable and tested business *and* also to increase competition, so that NASA could be sure to have alternatives to choose from, while doing all it could to work with the best. Designing procurement to achieve this was the challenge!

The design of contracts to strengthen NASA's negotiating position became an important factor inside the organization. Originally NASA used cost-plus contracts (CPFF), paying business for all costs plus a fee as profit. This created problems, as the contractor was not penalized for underbidding or for bad performance and poor management that could lead to excessive costs – indeed, there was no incentive to reduce costs at all. NASA later moved to a fixed-price model with incentives to increase both performance and efficiency. While CPFF meant that profits and performance were not linked, fixed-price contracts instead forced business to be more efficient and perform as well as possible, with extra incentives to meet specific criteria (e.g. speed). The incentives were designed to increase quality and performance and avoid cutting corners to achieve low costs. Getting the right 'deal' with business and eliminating rent-seeking led NASA in 1962 to add a 'no excess profits' clause in its contracts. Profits were fine, but space should not become a speculative affair, driven by overcharging and by companies more competent in 'brochuremanship' (whose descendant is the shiny PowerPoint of modern-day consulting companies) than getting the job done.

Work with external contractors was carried out with firm and nimble direction from NASA, and with attention to what should and should not be outsourced. Internal capabilities and expertise were seen as essential in negotiating proper contracts. Contracts were designed to be clear about goals, but allowed for freedom on how to achieve them; indeed, project goals and contract definition occurred together, as the contract was part of the design of mission governance. The key role of NASA is to define the mission, plan the programme, be clear on the guidelines, set the parameters, and then allow as much innovation as possible to create the product or service required. None of this could have been done without the NASA staff themselves having experience of the underlying science and technology; in fact, it would have been impossible to choose contractors intelligently without that knowledge. Additionally, by developing internal expertise, contracts with the private sector, once made, would be better managed because those writing them would know just as much about the technology as the contractor – and they could avoid 'capture'. Indeed, in-house R&D in research institutions in Lewis, Langley or Goddard was undertaken specifically so that NASA civil servants would be up to speed with the development of technology, giving them the level of confidence and knowledge necessary to keep contractors at arm's length. This was also seen as a way to attract talent: top scientists would not want to work in NASA if they could not get their hands dirty, or as Wernher von Braun put it, 'to keep in touch with the hardware and its problems'. In modern-day business-school speak, this means retaining 'absorptive capacity', i.e. the need to invest internally in knowledge creation so as to understand and interact dynamically with external opportunities when they arise.[29] In 1962, a Report to the President organized by Budget Director David Bell clearly said: 'There are certain functions which should under no circumstances be contracted out. The management and control of the Federal research and development effort must be firmly in the hands of full-time Government officials clearly responsible to the President and Congress.'[30]

The Apollo spacecraft programme was the outcome not only of public investment but also a lot of commercially minded private investments (see Figure 3 below). For example, General Motors spent $15.9 million ($100.4 million in 2019 terms) on developing the service propulsion fuel and oxidizer tanks. Pratt and Whitney (then United Aircraft) spent $95.1 million ($600.3 million) on building fuel cell powerplants. Aerojet Rocketdyne (the Aerojet Liquid Rocket Co.) spent $117.6 million ($742.4 million) on the service propulsion engine. And Honeywell spent $141.3 million ($892 million) on the stabilization and control subsystem.

The LEM is an outstanding example of how partnership

Figure 3 (*opposite*): Private-sector investments for Apollo launch vehicles

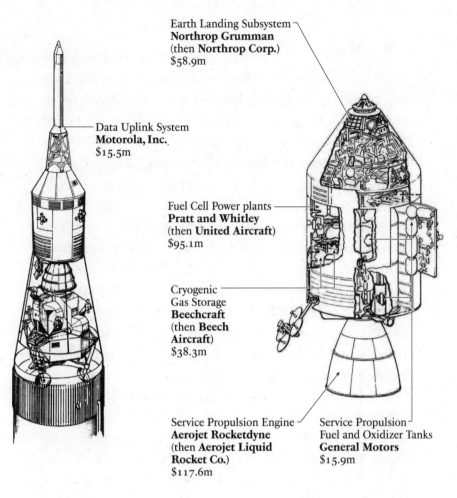

Earth Landing Subsystem
Northrop Grumman
(then **Northrop Corp.**)
$58.9m

Data Uplink System
Motorola, Inc.
$15.5m

Fuel Cell Power plants
Pratt and Whitley
(then **United Aircraft**)
$95.1m

Cryogenic
Gas Storage
Beechcraft
(then **Beech
Aircraft**)
$38.3m

Service Propulsion Engine
Aerojet Rocketdyne
(then **Aerojet Liquid
Rocket Co.**)
$117.6m

Service Propulsion
Fuel and Oxidizer Tanks
General Motors
$15.9m

Mechanical Timers
and Clocks
Hammond Organ Co.
$3.2m

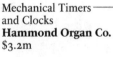

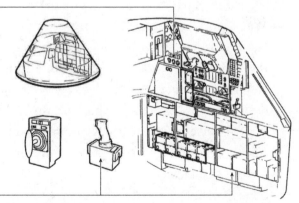

Stabilization and
Control Subsystem
Honeywell
$141.3m

with business worked how and clear needs and priorities in NASA stimulated innovation in the private sector. The LEM was a unique engineering feat and one of the truly state-of-the-art technologies the Apollo programme developed. When, in 1962, NASA awarded the contract to build the LEM to the then Grumman Aircraft Engineering Corporation, the company had never built anything like it before.

Images of people flying in space conjure up something sleek and sexy. The LEM was neither. It did not even look like something intended to fly. Yet the LEM was the ultimate in form following function. Everything that contributed to the impression of an ungainly machine had a purpose. Unlike the CSM, the LEM didn't need to be aerodynamic because it would never fly in earth's atmosphere. Resembling an insect, it had two tiny, triangular windows for eyes looking in different directions, a gaping mouth, a multifaceted top with an array of antennae and a more symmetrical lower half with four dangling legs.

This LEM, which eventually flew, was a distant descendent of Grumman's early designs. At the beginning, Grumman didn't understand how to go about the task. The company had earned its reputation making military aircraft during World War Two. Their initial design was largely inspired by helicopters. It had smooth surfaces, two large glass bubbles for the astronauts to look out through and comfortable seats. NASA's contract weight was 24,500 pounds and the initial design started out at 22,000 pounds. But, on seeing the design, NASA rejected it outright. Grumman had neglected to consider contingency back-up systems, never mind the back-ups for the back-ups. Getting a man to the moon was the main objective, but safety was the highest priority.

The back-up systems complicated the job considerably and the LEM's weight roughly doubled. Grumman had to go back to the drawing board to meet NASA's stringent demands for weight, safety and reliability. The company had to stop thinking like a plane manufacturer and start thinking like a spacecraft manufacturer. Out went the glass bubbles – too heavy – and out went the seats. As the space programme developed, NASA added new requirements, which increased the weight: computer navigation, the lunar buggy to transport astronauts over the moon's surface, equipment for experiments to be carried out on the moon.

Grumman also had to build the highly specialist facility to assemble and test the vehicle. It had pressurized rooms that were cleaner than an operating theatre to minimize dust or tiny pieces of metal that could short electrical circuits. But weight continued to be the greatest concern: every ounce saved meant more time to hover over the moon's surface when looking for a place to land. Grumman had to develop and refine its approach again and again. Solutions had to be found which pushed the technology of the day to its limits. For example, the outer shell of the vehicle was exceptionally thin – 0.03 centimetres, as thin as an aluminium can or a piece of paper. Buzz Aldrin in his memoirs joked that he could have punctured it with a pen.

Charlie Duke, one of the astronauts who flew the LEM, described the vehicle as being like a helicopter only with a rocket engine instead of rotor blades. In order to give the spacecraft the ability to hover and move in all directions, the rocket engine had to be capable of variable, controlled flight. Grumman engineers needed to build an engine that was simple and utterly reliable, able to start, stop and be throttled to regulate altitude, direction and speed.

As the date for the first flight tests of the LEM approached towards the end of 1968, Grumman was still a long way from achieving the weight reductions necessary. It was clear that radical action was needed. The company introduced new management systems, creating Action Centers where day-to-day changes could be monitored on big boards. At one point, Grumman was spending $10,000 for every pound of weight saved. New machining techniques were developed to chemically etch certain metal surfaces to further reduce weight. In the end the vehicle flew at about 33,000 pounds. In a remarkable tribute to the innovation NASA had stimulated, the LEM was immensely reliable and worked on all six of the lunar landings and take-offs between 1969 and 1972.

The nature of missions in NASA has changed over time, and with it the relationship between public and private actors. While military motives dominated in the 1950s and 1960s, the aim since the 1980s has been mostly to improve economic and competitive positions. In 1979, NASA administrator Robert Frosch set the stage for a more interactive relationship with the private sector by creating the 'NASA Guidelines Regarding Early Usage of Space for Industrial Purposes'. President Reagan's administration further developed commercialization within its National Space Policy. In 1984, he established the NASA Office of Commercial Programs and the Commercial Space Launch Act, which aimed to streamline the 'unnecessarily complicated' process of approving private-sector space endeavours.[31] The Commercial Space Act, passed by Congress in 1998, identified the economic development of 'earth orbital space' as a key priority of the International Space Station, embedding commercialization directly into NASA's mission.

This shift in priorities has coincided with the explicitly stated objective that public funding should have clear commercial outcomes. This more recent period has also seen the introduction of intermediary organizations like the Center for the Advancement of Science in Space (CASIS), to manage R&D and partnerships between NASA and the private sector – exactly the intermediation that NASA officials shunned during the Apollo years, as they thought that without internal skills and experience in project management, NASA would lose its way.

The priority for commercialization has affected the goals of government research funding, causing agencies like NASA – but also others like DARPA and the NIH – to have to justify the success of research by proving, or providing a convincing argument for, the 'economic value' of their science and technology bases.[32] Ironically, this focus on short-term economic value metrics, such as jobs created in business, leads to less commercialization than mission-oriented policies, as the latter have had such strong commercial spillovers.[33] So commercialization becomes easier when you don't worry about it. A valuable lesson is that partnership and common purpose can be dissipated as well as created.

There is a larger lesson. What if government, instead of being viewed as cumbersome while the private sector takes the risks, bears the greatest level of uncertainty and reforms its internal organization to take such risks? Imagine the transformation: from a bureaucratic top-down administration to a goal-oriented stimulator of new ideas from the ground up. Imagine government transformed across the board, from how procurement operates, to how research grants are made, to how public loans are structured and costs and budgeting are understood – all *to fulfil public purpose*. If we could think and act in this way, we could realize a new vision for sustainable cities or inspire business investment in the social infra-structure and health-care innovations required for a new understanding of well-being, or tackle the greatest challenges of our time such as climate change and health pandemics.

PART III: MISSIONS IN ACTION

What grand challenges we should tackle today

5: Aiming Higher: Mission-oriented Policies on Earth

The moon landing brought public and private actors together to solve one of the hardest problems humanity had ever set itself. The challenge was 'beat the Russians in space!'. But it was the setting of a clear, ambitious and urgent goal with a deadline – get a man on the moon and back in a decade! – that catalysed innovation and collaboration in a wide variety of different sectors. It took hundreds of project-based solutions to fulfil the mission, which required risk-taking, trial and error, and many failures along the way.

How do we apply these same 'mission' principles to the most pressing problems on earth today – making sure the missions themselves are ambitious and grounded in making the lives of people better? Moonshots must be understood not as siloed big endeavours, perhaps the pet project of a minister, but rather as bold societal goals which can be achieved by collaboration on a large scale between public and private entities. Today's missions need to be nested on top of resilient systems and social and physical infrastructure. The Apollo programme would have never worked had the military-industrial complex not been its backbone.

There is certainly no lack of challenges that need a mission-oriented approach. The UN's Sustainable Development Goals (SDGs, in Figure 4) outline seventeen of the greatest problems

Figure 4 (*following pages*): Seventeen UN Sustainable Development Goals

Seventeen UN Sustainable Development Goals

On 25 September 2015, countries adopted a set of goals to end poverty, protect the planet, and ensure prosperity for all as part of a new sustainable development agenda. Each goal has specific targets to be achieved over the next 15 years.

Goal 1.
End poverty in all its forms everywhere

Goal 2.
End hunger, achieve food security and improved nutrition and promote sustainable agriculture

Goal 3.
Ensure healthy livers and promote well-being for all at all ages

Goal 4.
Ensure inclusive and equitable quality education and promote lifelong learning oportunities for all

Goal 5.
Achieve gender equality and empower all women and girls

Goal 6.
Ensure availability and sustainable management of water and sanitation for all

Goal 7.
Ensure access to affordable, reliable, sustainable and modern energy for all

Goal 8.
Promote sustained, inclusive and sustainable economic growth, full and productive employment and decent work for all

Goal 9.
Build resilient infrastructure, promote inclusive and sustainable industrialization and foster innovation

Goal 10.
Reduce inequality within and among countries

Goal 11.
Make cities and human settlements inclusive, safe, resilient and sustainable

Goal 12.
Ensure sustainable consumption and production patterns

Goal 13.
Take urgent action to combat climate change and its impacts

Goal 14.
Conserve and sustainably use the oceans, seas and marine resources for sustainable development

Goal 15.
Protect, restore and promote sustainable use of terrestrial ecosystems, sustainably manage forests, combat desertification, and halt and reverse land degradation and biodiversity loss

Goal 16.
Promote peaceful and inclusive societies for sustainable development, provide access to justice for all and build effective, accountable and inclusive institutions at all levels

Goal 17.
Strengthen the means of implementation and revitalize the Global Partnership for Sustainable Development

THE GLOBAL GOALS
For Sustainable Development

we have, from cleaning our oceans, reducing poverty and hunger to achieving greater gender equity – problems that are not just technological but also deeply political, requiring regulatory and behavioural change. In this sense they are even more challenging than the moon landing.

In his seminal work *The Moon and the Ghetto*,[1] the economist Richard Nelson posed a demanding question that reminds us of Ralph Abernathy's speech on 15 July 1969, cited earlier. Nelson asked why our innovation systems have achieved such difficult feats as landing a man on the moon, yet continue to be so terribly disorganized and technologically unsavvy in dealing with the earthly issues of poverty, illiteracy and the persistence of ghettos and slums. He argued that, while politics is partly the culprit, the real reason is that a purely scientific and technological solution could not solve such problems. Nelson was right. Social problems are 'wicked' in the way that social, political, technological and behavioural factors intersect. It is impossible to get greener cities, for example, without making many different changes in regulations, in citizen behaviours, and in incentives to use cleaner materials. In that sense, the moonshot was easier. One could argue that the first-generation of mission-oriented policies followed a 'big science meets big problems' maxim that worked spectacularly well in some instances (e.g. the space race). In others, it created inertia or, worse, long-term problems (e.g. nuclear energy). Applying mission-oriented thinking in our times requires not just adaptation but also institutional innovations that create new markets and reshape the existing ones. And, importantly, it also requires citizen participation.

This raises two issues that are key for a mission and the vision behind it. The first is: whose vision should determine it (i.e. who decides)? The moon landing, as inspirational as it was, was run from the top down by a white elite. This surely is not what will get us to achieve social goals in inequality and climate change. The second is that it might be easier to rouse approval for purely technological missions as opposed to those that are more social, like fighting climate change, which no doubt face more resistance. Indeed, the vision behind achieving carbon neutrality has been a feature of many progressive governments – but also a reason why they subsequently lost elections. This was the case in Australia in 2019, when the Labour Party put climate change at the heart of its manifesto, but it backfired due to the lack of support by those that feared it would cause unemployment. Thus having a vision is not enough: it is essential to engage with citizens about it. We will come back to this point at the end of the chapter.

Sustainable Development Goals and a green transition

The UN's SDGs set out today's challenges and cover areas such as poverty, hunger, climate and gender equality. The ambition is to achieve them all by 2030. They provide the perfect starting point for considering the challenges that missions might address.[2]

One strength of the SDGs is that they engage diverse stakeholders across the world. They identify internationally agreed grand challenges that have been chosen by broad and comprehensive consultation around the world. They offer huge opportunities to direct innovation at multiple social and technological problems to create societies that are just, inclusive and sustainable. Another strength is that the SDGs address complex and cross-sector problems. They involve much more than technological change. They are problems without straightforward solutions, and so they require a better understanding of how social issues interact with political and technological ones, behavioural changes and critical feedback processes. Because of this complexity, it is important to break the challenges down into practical steps or targets.

The targets under the SDGs – 169 of them! – require specific innovations and hence experimentation by different actors. They fit very nicely into a mission-oriented approach, where the challenge is only solved through experimentation around many projects that together complete the mission. (Recall the hundreds of problems that needed solving before getting to the moon.) Consider 'SDG 7: Affordable and Clean Energy' as an example. This goal has three targets to reach by 2030: ensure universal access to affordable, reliable and modern energy services; increase substantially the share of renewable energy in the global energy mix; and double the global rate of improvement in energy efficiency. Similarly, 'SDG 5: Gender Equality' has six targets: (1) end all forms of discrimination against all women and girls everywhere; (2) eliminate all forms of violence against women and girls in the public and private spheres, including trafficking and sexual and other types of exploitation; (3) eliminate all harmful practices, such as child, early and forced marriage and female genital mutilation; (4) recognize and value unpaid care and domestic work through the provision of public services, infrastructure and social protection policies and the promotion of shared responsibility within the household and the family as nationally appropriate; (5) ensure women's full and effective participation and equal opportunities for leadership at all levels of decision-making in political, economic and public life; and (6) ensure universal access to sexual and reproductive health and reproductive rights as agreed in accordance with the UN Programme of Action of the International Conference on Population and Development (1994), the Beijing Platform for Action from the Fourth World Conference on Women (1995) and the outcome documents from their review conferences.

A moonshot approach to real-world problems is neither utopian nor easy. In recent years I have directly participated in this complex process, helping to bring the missions concept to the fore of policymaking globally. This chapter reflects on some of the lessons from this experience.

In 2017–18 I helped the European Commission apply a mission-oriented approach to its innovation policy. While the EC had talked generally about challenge-led policy, such as policies aimed at 'smart, inclusive and sustainable growth', what was missing was a clear pathway for that to happen. And while innovation policy was focused on outcomes – such as support for specific technologies or the encouragement of start-ups – the policies together were not producing the transformational shifts needed for growth. I argued that this was because the logic needed to reverse: the focus should be on problems that innovation can solve, and the technology and start-ups would follow. After all, the internet itself did not arise from a focus on computing but from the need to get satellites to communicate. My work with the EC led to two reports explaining how a mission-oriented approach could be mapped, one on what a mission-oriented approach is about, and the second on how to 'govern' missions at the policy level.[3]

The idea behind a *mission map* is that you begin by asking: what is the problem you want to solve? You then frame it as a goal that catalyses investment and innovation in many different sectors and inspires new collaborations at the project level. Figure 5 illustrates the approach: from challenge to mission to sectoral investments with specific projects underlying them.[4] On the basis of these reports, missions became a legal instrument in the EU innovation programme (the Horizon Programme), and after long political negotiation with the EC, five mission areas were selected. After their selection, there was an opportunity for stakeholders to respond across European society (business, academia, civil society and policymakers). Figure 6 lists the five

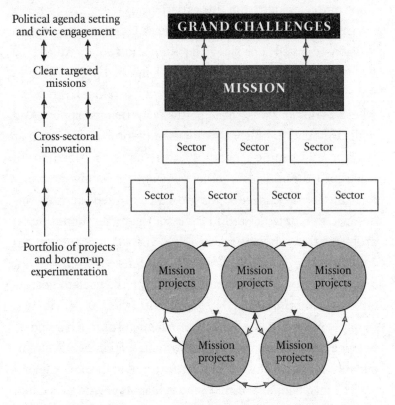

Figure 5: A mission map

- Adaptation to **climate change** including societal transformation
- **Cancer**
- **Healthy oceans,** seas, coastal and inland waters
- Climate-neutral and **smart cities**
- **Soil health** and **food**

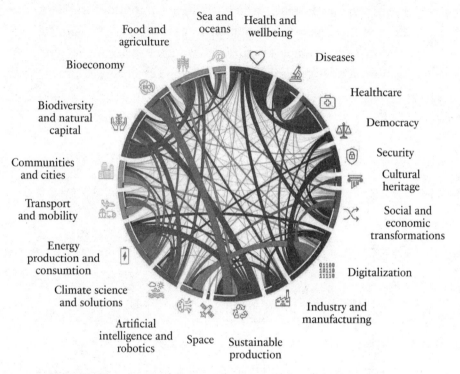

Figure 6: Five mission areas selected by the EU (and interconnections)

mission areas, while also showing their interconnections across sectors in the economy.

At the time of writing, specific missions are being framed within each area. The cancer mission is not just about reducing cancer rates but also addresses the types of policies and investments that can improve the quality of life of cancer survivors. The oceans mission looks not only at cleaning up the seas, but also at restoring damaged ecosystems. And the mission areas of course intersect: the soil and food mission, which tries to render the entire value chain of food production more sustainable, will necessarily interact with the mission on climate and clean growth.

Targets need to foster as much cross-sector innovation and investment as possible, which is why it's important to frame them widely and inspire ambition. Let's take 'SDG 13: Climate Action' as an example (Figure 7). Using the mission-mapping framework, we can break down the grand challenge of climate

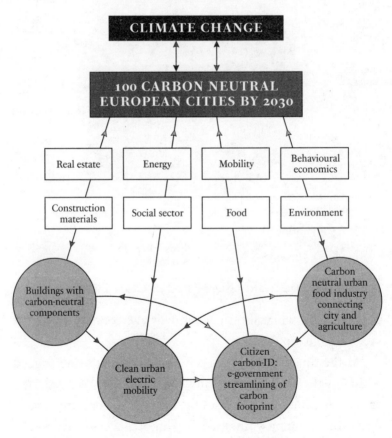

Figure 7: A mission map for 'Climate Action' (SDG 13)

action into a mission to build 100 carbon-neutral cities across Europe. A mission of this sort would involve innovations in multiple areas, from citizens' mobility patterns to e-governance, transport infrastructure, nutrition and construction standards. The mission projects would potentially include fully electrifying the public transport system; creating carbon-absorbing materials for the construction industry; producing carbon-ID cards for all citizens so that each person can monitor his or her carbon footprint; and finding new ways for food systems in cities to link to locally produced organic agriculture in the countryside.

We can find another application of mission mapping in 'SDG 14: Life below Water' (Figure 8), a goal that focuses on the disastrous proliferation of plastic in our seas and oceans. Ridding our oceans of plastic is a massive undertaking, and not only for the marine sector: it must also involve other sectors too like design, new materials, waste management and behavioural psychology.[4] By mapping it we can see how this targeted mission could spawn hundreds of projects, from biodegradable plastic substitutes to innovations in image recognition and autonomous plastic removal mechanisms in oceans.

In this diagram, the circles represent the projects that happen on the ground. The arrows connecting the circles represent new conversations and collaborations between project communities. For policymakers, the main point is to use policy instruments – such as prize schemes, grants and loans – to foster as much creative thinking as possible at the project level, and also to join up initiatives so that the sum is greater than the parts.

This raises the question of whether missions should be led by their own agencies, much as NASA led the moonshot mission. The DARPA model of an innovation agency, with risk-taking, experimentation and portfolio management built

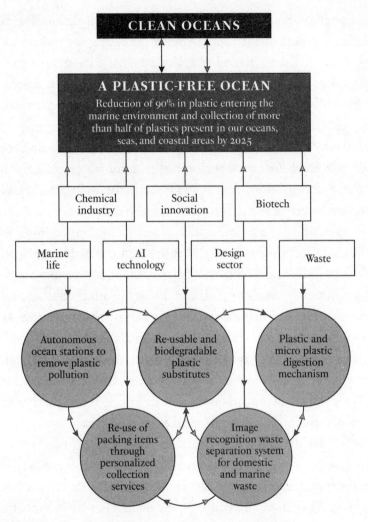

Figure 8: A mission map for 'Life below Water' (SDG 14)

into its structure, remains the target. But without such agencies, the EC has had to invent its own.

For now, the EC has decided on 'mission boards' to bring leadership and rigour to its five mission areas. The mission boards advise the EC on concrete missions within their mission area, and afterwards advise on implementation-related issues. While the key idea is to change the normal approach of keeping a wide agenda that will serve everyone to making real choices around specific missions with significant resources, this is easier said than done. Experts in the mission boards were selected to make the choice and give legitimacy to that choice. The risk is that there is little appetite to make choices as everyone defends their own corner.

It is still uncertain whether the EC will hire external partners to implement the mission – use a third party that will receive the funding and which will run the calls for projects. This, of course, is very different from creating mission-oriented agencies in-house – of the DARPA kind – and could raise problems such as those mentioned above, when core government activities are outsourced. Ideally the risks would be taken inside the EC, with the development of capacity and capabilities related to mission-oriented policy. But this requires making missions work across the EC departments (DGs), which is currently not so easy given the complexity and 'silos' across the DGs.

In 2017, I also advised the UK government on how to apply a mission-oriented approach to its industrial strategy. This led to the creation of the 2017 *Industrial Strategy: Building a Britain fit for the future*,[5] which concentrated on four challenges: the future of mobility, clean growth, healthy ageing and artificial intelligence and the data economy. On the back of this, I set up and co-chaired a Commission for Mission-Oriented Innovation and Industrial Strategy (MOIIS) to help the UK government turn each of the four chosen challenges into concrete missions – a process that involved working for over a year with dozens of civil servants. Together we created mission maps for each challenge: for

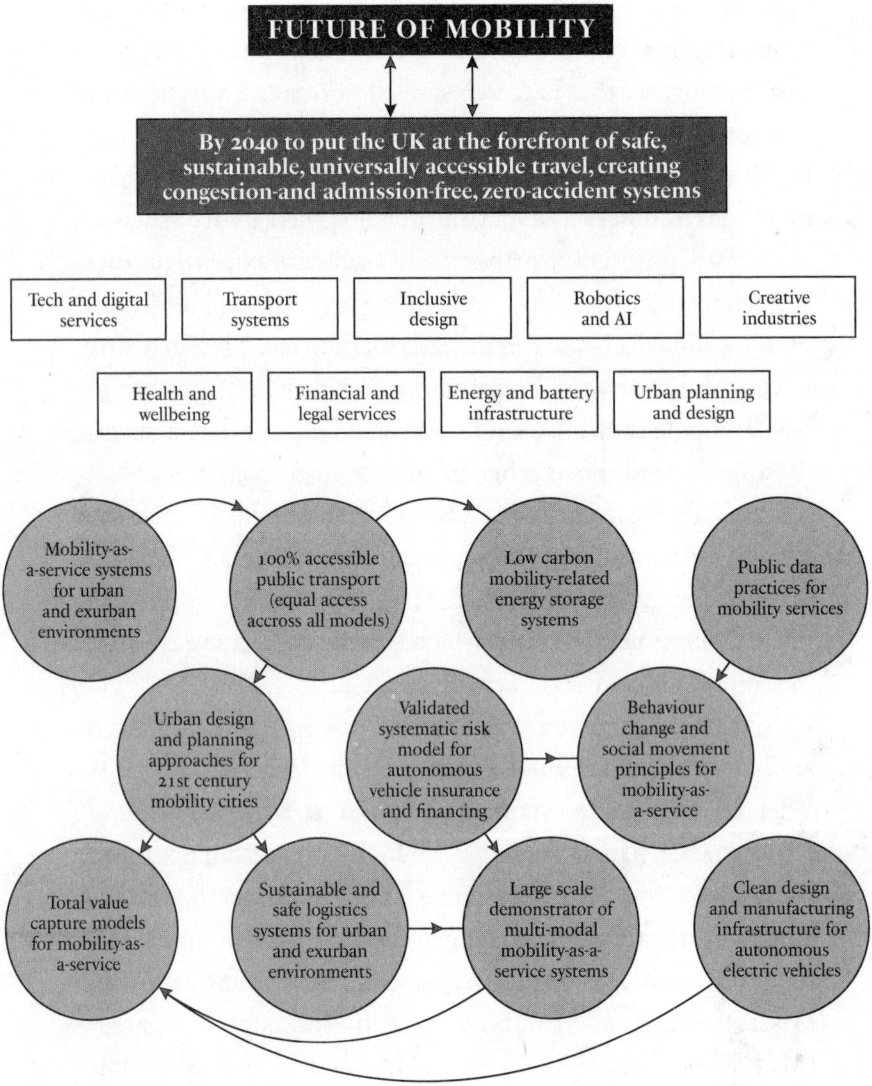

FUTURE OF MOBILITY

By 2040 to put the UK at the forefront of safe, sustainable, universally accessible travel, creating congestion-and admission-free, zero-accident systems

| Tech and digital services | Transport systems | Inclusive design | Robotics and AI | Creative industries |

| Health and wellbeing | Financial and legal services | Energy and battery infrastructure | Urban planning and design |

Mobility-as-a-service systems for urban and exurban environments

100% accessible public transport (equal access accross all models)

Low carbon mobility-related energy storage systems

Public data practices for mobility services

Urban design and planning approaches for 21st century mobility cities

Validated systematic risk model for autonomous vehicle insurance and financing

Behaviour change and social movement principles for mobility-as-a-service

Total value capture models for mobility-as-a-service

Sustainable and safe logistics systems for urban and exurban environments

Large scale demonstrator of multi-modal mobility-as-a-service systems

Clean design and manufacturing infrastructure for autonomous electric vehicles

Figure 9: A mission map for the 'Future of Mobility'

example, the future of mobility challenge (Figure 9) was designed as ambitiously as possible to stimulate innovation across different sectors, from transport to digital to finance and health. And by being ambitious around 'universally accessible travel', we tried to encourage innovation around areas such as disabilities: there isn't only one way to get up a ramp. Similarly, we worked on an ambitious mission which looked at healthy living in people's later years, with individual projects related to battling loneliness and the potential decline in self-worth (Figure 10).

That same year, I worked closely with the First Minister of Scotland to set up a new public bank that put missions at its core, the Scottish National Investment Bank. Key to this work was creating an institution dedicated to long-term finance but which did not just provide handouts to companies which asked for them. Rather, it was directed to back companies that were willing to engage with society-wide goals, such as the ability of the health service to engage more actively with the opportunities presented by 'big' data and digitalization. In this sense the bank's mission was to create a portfolio of investments that 'picked the willing'.

Achieving missions in modern society is not easy, as it means changing much of what we take for granted about how government works. For one thing, it requires government to work across its usual silos. A clean growth mission will necessarily involve the Department of Transport, the Department of Business, Energy and Industrial Strategy, the Department of Industry, Innovation and Science – and, of course, the

Figure 10 (*following page*): A mission map for 'Healthy Ageing'

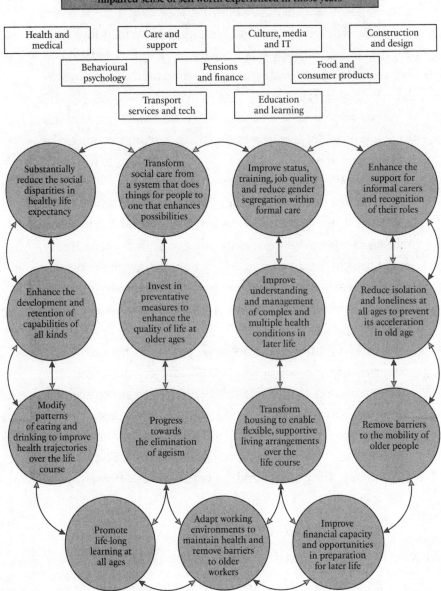

Treasury. It also requires changing fundamental habits such as what we eat and how we move. None of that can happen without government learning how to engage with citizens in genuine (rather than tokenistic) way.

Indeed, this is a key lesson for innovation in general. While explicit innovation budgets are often housed in a department/ministry of innovation or industry, innovation needs to be part of how government operates every day – including how it purchases goods and services across all its departments. This allows innovation to trickle through the procurement budgets, which might be four times as large in one department as the entire innovation budget among departments.

Thus, working interdepartmentally can help reveal the full scale of government procurement and leverage a much higher budget for missions. Seeing government as *purchaser* is the best way to increase any innovation budget. And that comes from having a clear vision for change: innovative thinking can drive how you build a bridge, a school or a motorway.

What follows are the key considerations for taking a mission-oriented approach, from selecting and implementing a mission to engaging the public.

Selecting a mission

First and foremost, a mission has to be bold and inspirational while having wide societal relevance. It must be clear in its intention to develop ambitious solutions that will directly improve people's daily lives, and it should appeal to the imagination. As we saw with the SDGs, missions also need to have clear direction that is measurable and time-bound, which comes from setting a concrete target with a specific timeframe. This target can be formulated in binary ways (for example, a man reaches the moon and returns back safely) or in quantifiable ways (for example, changes to manufacturing to reduce carbon emissions by 30 per cent in five years), and can be evaluated by asking a single question: 'Did we achieve it or not?' This is how to determine the success or failure of a mission and measure progress along the way.

A mission also needs to set goals for investment and innovation that are ambitious but realistic. It's important to take risks and push civil servants, researchers and innovators to deliver above and beyond what they normally would. But their goals must be feasible, at least in theory, within the given time period. Finding the right balance is key: objectives that are unrealistic won't gain sufficient buy-in, while ones that lack ambition will not inspire effort or investment.

The technology required to achieve those objectives should also attract research and innovation activities that private actors would not otherwise undertake. Indeed, a mission should spur innovation across multiple disciplines (including social sciences and humanities), across different sectors (such as transport, nutrition, health, services), and across different types of actors (public, private, third-sector, civil-society organizations). It does this by focusing on a problem that affects multiple sectors and opens up the possibility for system-wide transformation.

People often look to DARPA as a way to consider organizational innovation inside the public sector. DARPA – the key investor in the internet as well as innovations like Siri – has always been mission-driven and known for its ability to attract top talent even without paying the kinds of salaries offered, for example, by the Singapore government (up to $1 million for department heads), so attraction to the project means more than money. This mission mystique is determined by a strong sense of purpose, such as to win a war or implement a Green New Deal. It is also determined by the ability to invest, lead and create with confidence, words usually applied only to business leaders. Key to DARPA's model has been the explicit recognition that internal ways of working must be flexible and adaptive.

DARPA is the perfect example of why it is wrong to think that government is simply there to de-risk private risk-takers. DARPA took enormous risks in funding the invention of the internet – and it did so with a problem in mind: so that satellites could communicate. Similarly, the US Navy funded the invention of GPS in an effort to target missiles better. The point is: to think in a mission-oriented way is revolutionary because it requires rethinking the role of government in the economy, putting purpose first and solving problems that are important to citizens. It means transforming government from being merely an 'enabler' or even a 'stifler' of innovation to becoming the engine of innovation. Usually this type of flexibility and outcomes orientation only occurs in wartime, when military organizations are given autonomy from more bureaucratic branches of government. And yet DARPA works in peacetime, too. Recently, for example, DARPA funded early R&D for two pharmaceutical companies, Moderna Inc. and Inovio Pharmaceutical Inc., to create RNA and DNA vaccines – technologies that many scientists and investors considered speculative and high-risk. However, DARPA believed that nucleic-acid-based vaccines could be developed much faster than conventional technologies, and their bet paid off. In 2020, after the COVID-19 pandemic hit, Moderna's RNA vaccine became the first COVID-19 vaccine to be administered in a Phase I trial, and Inovio's DNA-based vaccine was on track to start a Phase I trial shortly thereafter. Pursuing high-risk, high-reward technologies is routine for DARPA, which continually creates, manufactures and distributes prophylactics within sixty days of identifying a new viral pathogen.

And this leads to the final consideration for selecting a mission: it needs to encourage multiple solutions instead of focusing on a single development path or technology. While missions are targeted towards a specific goal, the goal should be broad enough to encompass numerous projects that together achieve the overall mission. Some of these projects will fail; others will succeed. But the ambition is to stimulate as many different ideas and routes to solutions as possible. Missions are a way to implement directionality inside an economy. But, as discussed in the Introduction, redirection will not work if it is not aligned across policy areas. So while missions are key, the surrounding tax and fiscal space needs to be aligned as well.

Implementing a mission

To solve specific problems that catalyse investment and collaboration between many different people and organizations, we need policy instruments that focus on outcomes and foster experimentation. Procurement contracts, grants, loans and prize schemes should reward innovators for taking risks to solve public problems, whether the aim is to develop a vaccine or a new way to help hospitals share data. This means putting less emphasis on the need to support specific types of firms (such as SMEs and start-ups), less on specific technologies (such as 'high-tech', artificial intelligence, quantum computing), and less on specific sectors to promote (such as life sciences or the creative sector). At the same time, it means putting more emphasis on the big problems facing society and how all types of organizations, technologies and sectors can play a role in solving them.

Prize schemes, in particular, are useful for driving cross-sector innovation – and have been for hundreds of years. In 1675, the Royal Observatory was founded at Greenwich, on the River Thames to the east of London, to carry out astronomical observations. Part of the Observatory's mission was to help with the thorny problem of how to measure longitude – the distance east or west of the prime meridian which runs north to south through the Observatory and girdles the globe. Determining longitude was becoming critical for commercial and naval reasons. Britain was locked in competition with rival powers, notably France and Holland. Ships were being lost, or their voyages were taking longer than necessary, because they could not accurately establish their position at sea. Being able to work out longitude would give a country a commercial and naval advantage.

Impressively, the announcement of the Longitude Prize eventually led to two solutions being developed simultaneously. John Harrison, a self-taught working-class clockmaker, used his great mechanical talent and determination to build a series of marine timekeepers, culminating in the model called H4. After years of wrangling with the Board of Longitude, he eventually won a total of £23,065, more than £3 million in today's money. The H4 later became known as the marine chronometer and can still be seen in the Greenwich

Observatory. In addition, the British mathematician John Hadley and the German astronomer Tobias Mayer improved and perfected the mechanisms and tables necessary to use the lunar distance method effectively. The work of the Astronomer Royal, Nevil Maskelyne, at the Royal Observatory proved how timekeeping methods and astronomical observations can complement each other and lead to successful determination of longitude. Today, the Longitude Prize is structured as a £10 million prize fund, with an £8 million payout, that will reward a team of researchers who develop a point-of-care diagnostic test which will conserve antibiotics for future generations and revolutionize the delivery of global health care. The test must be accurate, rapid, affordable and easy to use anywhere in the world.

Along with new policy instruments, missions need a new approach to governance. New kinds of governance include financing operations differently so that public finance is seen as an investor of first resort, not just a lender of last resort. The public sector can crowd in private investment and increase the 'multiplier effect' (i.e. how much activity is stimulated by each dollar or euro of government investment) by shaping perceptions of future opportunities. But it requires building new capabilities in public institutions – including redesigning procurement contracts to foster new ideas for solving problems – and changing government culture so it is less risk-averse and more open to portfolios containing a wide array of ambitious projects.[6] Financial institutions themselves can become more mission-oriented by directing public finance towards societal goals – be they public banks or sovereign wealth funds. Too often such funds end up simply doling out money to pet projects or firms seen as particularly in need of support, such as small and mid-size enterprises. It is crucial instead to demonstrate more ambition and provide patient, long-term finance to organizations willing and able to help steer an economy towards meeting its challenges.

Financing missions can be complex. The amount of funding is obviously important. Less obvious is the importance of providing the right kind of funding at the right stage in the evolution of a mission. This is especially true where a mission involves a high degree of risky innovation.

There is a large and diverse network of institutions and types of financing which together make up a public–private ecosystem. On the public side are research funding, public venture capital funds and procurement policies aimed at SMEs and national and regional development banks such as Kreditanstalt für Wiederaufbau (KfW) in Germany and the European Investment Bank. With missions in mind, the EC has introduced a European Innovation Council, dedicated programme managers and blended finance of grants and equity investments to help breakthrough innovations. Procurement to solve public goals, including the production of ventilators during a health pandemic, can be used to drive innovation in business – with the focus on the goal rather than static metrics around commercialization. The key is to specify what is needed without micromanaging the way in which it is done – so to stimulate as much creativity and innovation in multiple actors.

On the private side, finance for innovation and missions runs the gamut from private venture capital to investment banks' innovation funds. But there are two major challenges. One is how to crowd in private sources of finance that are generally cautious. The other is how to share the risks and rewards fairly between the public and private sectors.

Understanding the spread of risk across the chain of innovation from its original concept to final commercial development helps to see how crowding in might work. A broad range of research and innovation coalesces around a mission and particular types of finance usually suit particular stages of innovation. Missions depend heavily on keeping the variety of financing as extensive and flexible as possible. For instance, grants may be most suitable for blue-sky early-stage research and innovation, while towards the other end of the spectrum equity capital can help technology companies scale up to fully commercial operation. Debt capital and long-term loans may be better for lower-risk activities. The structure of loans, grants and procurement contracts can be redesigned to enable experimentation, as can the form of policies themselves. The purpose is to secure *outcomes* and to avoid short-term budgetary pressures truncating or ending missions whose long-term benefits are immense.

To track and measure the progress of a mission, we need to use appropriate indicators and monitoring frameworks. This is the opposite of static CBA and net present value calculations (the difference between the present value of cash flows and the present value of cash flows over a certain period when adjusted for inflation), which are likely to strangle any bold mission at birth. Instead, we need to use flexible and dynamic metrics that capture, for example, the cross-sectoral spillovers that occur – often serendipitously – on the path to a mission. We also need to set intermediate milestones so that an agency can decide to stop subsidizing failing projects. Making real-time data publicly available can help create a sense of urgency, acknowledge achievement and encourage motivation about progress.

All of this depends on building in-house capabilities in public institutions that enable them to proactively manage a portfolio of projects. As we've seen, without these capabilities governments will resort to outsourcing work and knowledge to third parties such as consulting companies, think tanks and the private sector. Public organizations responsible for engaging with technological and scientific priorities must also invest in in-house scientific and technological expertise and nurture their capabilities and capacity for risk-taking and experimentation. And yet in many countries it is exactly these types of capabilities that have been either outsourced or simply cut.[7]

Which leads to the final point about implementing a mission: missions must change how the public and private sectors work together. This partnership is less about handouts, guarantees and assistance, and more about co-investment, sharing risks and sharing rewards. The private sector needs to work with the public sector to achieve society's goals: not through corporate social responsibility or charity, but through the value chain – where money is made while supporting society's aims – and through investment with public purpose.

A word of caution is needed here. The point of business and government working together is to achieve a common mission. It is not about government bringing in the private sector to show how public research leads to commercialization. Most commercialization opportunities from public research – such as the development of the software industry following Apollo – occurred precisely when government kept its eye on the prize and did not worry about the economic value or commercialization that would result. The objectives were clear, so that if the private sector did not deliver, it was sent back to the drawing board (remember Grumman).

Engaging citizens in a mission

The 1960s, when the Apollo programme took place, was a period still retaining much of the sense of community purpose that followed the rebuilding of Europe and the USA after World War Two. In addition, there was a common desire to reach a détente in the Cold War. However, from the mid 1970s onwards, the cultural norm in North America – and to a significant extent in the UK, although less so in Continental Europe – shifted from community obligations to individual rights. There were several reasons for this. A younger generation (the baby boomers) had only second-hand experience of the Depression and wartime privations. Increasing financialization, following deregulation of the financial sector, encouraged personal greed. And increasing prosperity and consumerism eroded the bonds of collective interest in favour of individual advancement.

Missions offer an opportunity to reverse this trend by involving citizens in solving grand societal challenges and creating wide civic excitement about the power of collective innovation. They present an appropriate time to put citizen participation at the heart of innovation policy and connect R&D and broader policy measures to issues that matter to people. Increasingly, social movements are influencing policy from the bottom up, even without a formal system of co-operation. Some missions, like Apollo, are launched from the very top; often, these are the missions that require a high scientific input. But missions that are as much social and political as technological require a much higher degree of citizen engagement. The movement for a 'Just Transition' is an example, whereby trade unions (especially) call for the transition to a green economy to include investment in helping workers adjust and share in the benefits – investing in green skills and capabilities, especially for workers losing jobs in the fossil-fuel sectors.[8]

A society's culture – in the sense of its creative culture and the broader sociological sense of what binds citizens together – can help citizens imagine a new way of life. For example, in 2017, David Attenborough, the renowned British naturalist and documentary maker, narrated a series called *Blue Planet II* on life in our seas and oceans. The last episode included heartwrenching scenes of baby dolphins choking and dying on the many small pieces of plastics that today infiltrate life below water. Children all over the world watched, and awareness of the urgent need for plastic-free oceans leapt up the public agenda way beyond conversations in small policy seminars or boardrooms. The concept of plastic-free oceans excited conversations in schools and around family dinner tables, underlining the power of culture and the creative sector more broadly in making missions understood and stimulating new activity.

Engaging and involving citizens in the design of missions has become, in some countries, a core principle of public-sector innovation, just as it is in innovative private-sector practice. There are many positive examples, notably in the generation of ideas and consultation that led to the framing of the SDGs. In discussions about the post-2015 Sustainable Development Agenda, people around the world aired their views through unprecedented consultation and the outreach efforts of organized civil-society groups, as well as through the global conversations led by the United Nations

Development Group on 'A Million Voices: The World We Want', 'Delivering the Post-2015 Agenda: Opportunities at the National and Local Levels' and the 'My World' survey. Co-design secures societal ownership of missions' goals, ensuring that missions enjoy a longevity that exceeds the period in which individual ministers or even governments are in office.

With the Apollo mission, citizens were inspired, but were not involved in designing the mission itself. That makes sense, of course, for purely technological missions. But for missions that are societal – linked to green growth, healthy living, the future of mobility or solving the digital divide – it is essential that different voices participate from the start to help think through the mission's implications for ordinary people and modify it to involve and benefit citizens as much as possible.

Policymakers need to be open to the frank debates that interactions with citizens might entail. For instance, the decades-long civic green movement has informed political concern about sustainable growth, as embodied in the *Energiewende* mission in Germany.[9] Meaning 'energy trans-formation', Energiewende is a mission backed by the German government to help address the challenge of climate change by reducing carbon emissions as well as dependency on nuclear power. Furthermore, when planning EU-wide innov-ation, citizen engagement must recognize Europe's diverse population and garner the views of under-represented groups, whether by age, class, race or other characteristics.

Sweden has been particularly active in setting place-based missions that use collaborative and participatory methods both within and across the system. Examples include a street-based mission to 'ensure every street in Sweden be healthy, sustainable and vibrant'. There are 40,000 km of streets in Sweden, which have often included more parking than living spaces. The idea is not only to build more living spaces but to do so with an ambitious notion of what it means to live together well. Another place-based mission is around school meals. The mission is to 'ensure every student eats healthy, sustainable and tasty school food'. Such a mission requires close collaboration between regional governments (where school food is procured) and the food agencies, local schools and farming organizations. The goal is to connect transformation within food systems to changes in education, local climate resilience and health care. Both the Streets mission and the School Food mission are examples of 'levers' that can be used to address SDGs, the national goal of a Fossil-free Sweden[10] and the 'viable city' strategy.[11] Involving local citizens in place-based missions is easier than in national ones. They can help set both the mission and the metrics to monitor whether it is being achieved: the students can confirm whether the school meals are indeed tasty!

Similarly, in a commission that I co-chair in London called the Camden Renewal Commission we have used the local housing estates to direct the borough's carbon-neutral ambitions. With a formidable set of expert Commissioners, including Michael Marmot, a leading UK expert in public health, George the Poet and Delia Barker, who directs the programme at Camden's Roundhouse theatre, we're building missions that are designed to embed sustainable, 'green' living in Camden's 270 estates, and to do so in a manner that galvanizes the creativity of those who live there. With green space set aside for intergenerational exchange, for play, learning and spontaneity, the mission aims for aesthetically pleasing, comfortable buildings where citizens are involved in budgeting decisions.

Establishing estates and streets as places where missions can root themselves makes for long-term citizen governance and stewardship, for the accumulation over time of public value and public innovation and ultimately for local prosperity and economic growth. At the time of writing, other missions in Camden are taking root in high streets, schools and other youth spaces.

The role of high streets as a 'bed' for missions is something I have explored previously, in collaboration with the Mayor of London's *High Streets Adaptive Strategies* project, in early 2019.[12] High streets are places where public and private investments meet citizens. Who are the streets for? How are the benefits distributed? Is the wealth created reinvested back into the streets or is it siphoned off? Setting missions at high-street level allows us to get to the heart of these questions, and to understand how public spaces and the public good need to be constantly contested and argued for.

High streets – from the famous commercial ones such as Glasgow's Buchanan Street, London's Oxford Street and Bath's Milsom Street, to the smaller local streets that serve neighbourhoods – can be powerful places to consider occupancy, interdependency, conditionality and co-operation between different stakeholders. How these elements act and interact within high streets as systems forms the basis for developing value in the public realm, and for creating missions that direct local economies in specific directions.

This openness towards citizens cannot be left to the goodwill of politicians but needs to be institutionalized and embedded over the long term. Using novel, online citizen consultation tools can help collect input from a large and broad group of people, cheaply and flexibly. Governments in Europe and beyond are keen to gain this kind of large-scale citizen feedback. For example, the EU-funded projects VOICES (Views, Opinions and Ideas of Citizens in Europe on Science) and CIMULACT (Citizen and Multi-Actor Consultation on Horizon 2020) aimed to engage citizens and stakeholders in the co-creation of European research agendas, such as Horizon 2020, based on real, validated and shared visions, needs and demands. These projects developed and experimented with long-term citizen participation and built capacities in existing methods. The experiments explored a variety of ways in which to test and inspire the research community with a broad range of options for engaging citizens and others in setting priorities for research and innovation. The diversity of methods also helped to target different societal groups, which enriched the feedback and validation of the research programme scenarios. In addition to online consultations, policymakers can also mine evidence on co-creation and citizen engagement from research and innovation projects that are publicly funded.

A significant challenge for the active involvement of any type of stakeholder group, including citizens or civil-society organizations, is avoiding the capture of missions by vested interests, and recognizing the differences between long-term civic needs and passing trends and phases. Citizens and their associations should work closely alongside policymakers, researchers and businesses: this will help all those involved to see issues from varied perspectives, avoid mission capture by any one group and bring about wider systemic change.

Finally, citizens should be engaged in the assessment of

missions. Citizen or civil-society organizations can be represented in evaluating proposals, reviewing the progress of projects, participating in advisory structures and generally making sure that the mission's outcomes are aligned with the needs, values and expectations of society. This, again, should take place alongside established researchers, businesses and policy experts with the assurance that all stakeholders act impartially. Transparency is also very important. To win and retain citizens' trust in tracking progress, public organizations implementing a mission-oriented research and innovation policy should commit to being transparent and applying an open data policy by subscribing to the FAIR principle (findable; accessible; interoperable; reusable).

In considering citizen engagement it is critical not to be deluded by the notion that it is harmonious. Many innovations that fundamentally altered the lives of citizens would have never come about without conflict and debate. The birth control pill would not have arisen without the feminist movement fighting for it. Similarly, HIV drugs would not have been devised without AIDS movements like ACT UP fighting for them, and we would not have the eight-hour workday or the weekend without the trade union movement, or women's votes without the Suffragettes.[13] Climate action groups such as Extinction Rebellion, building on several decades of growing and widespread environmental activism, are stepping up the pressure on governments, companies and citizens to act decisively to tackle the environmental emergency, from the wholesale transformation of energy and transport to banning plastic bags and packaging.

This is a key point, and one that merits reflection given also the resistance to the Apollo programme by those that were fighting for civil rights. The problem was not only the valid question – how could we spend so much on space with so many problems on earth? – but also, who was making the decisions? A vital aspect of a mission-oriented approach is to represent different people and perspectives, not just those of the 'elite' experts – often white males in their sixties. Recent thinking and political action around Black Lives Matter is about who defines what is valuable, and how that feeds back to biases, prejudices and racism – both explicit and hidden.

It also requires new governance frameworks. And for this reason it is interesting to consider the concept of stakeholder capitalism not only in terms of corporate governance (more on this in Chapter 6) but also in terms of governing transitions and missions. In recent times, citizen assemblies have also been used for democratic debate on big questions from Brexit in the U K to the green transition in Australia.

Mission: a Green New Deal

Greening the economy demands and deserves nothing less than a moonshot worthy of the mission. It is not a question of picking a series of outcomes that are only worthwhile for some market participants and disadvantage others. Solving climate change must be transformative across the entire economy. Public, private and civil actors alike will have to shift their mindset from short-term gains to long-run outcomes and profits, particularly against the background of financial stability and transition risks that form the landscape of climate change. Industrial strategies don't just need different goals: they need missions.

Imagine if we were to bring the courage, spirit of experimentation and willpower of the moonshot to bear on the greatest problem of our time: the climate emergency. Imagine having leaders who proudly declare: 'We choose to fight climate change in this decade not because it is easy, but because it is hard, because that goal will serve to organize and measure the best of our energies and skills, because that challenge is one that we are willing to accept, one we are unwilling to postpone, and one which we intend to win.'[14]

Around the world, there is increasing talk about the need for a Rooseveltian scale of investment to battle climate change. The notion of the Green New Deal consciously evokes the New Deal policies that began to lift the USA out of the Great Depression. A Green New Deal is about transforming production, distribution and consumption across the economy. It must be underpinned by long-term, patient finance which is willing to take risks and able to mobilize and crowd in other investors. This is key, as business investment reacts to the perception of where future opportunities lie: the climate emergency can be both a carrot and a stick to create a new direction of opportunities for the global economy. But where do we begin?

The mission map above on carbon-neutral cities (Figure 7) shows that a green transformation is not just about renewable energy. It's also about achieving a cross-sectoral approach to innovation whose goal is to build a diverse portfolio of mission projects that engage multiple sectors and spur experimentation by as many different types of organizations. Similarly, the mission map on the future of mobility (Figure 9) spans different sectors that could alter how citizens travel, from innovations in the way that disabled people access ramps to new forms of public transport, public data practices and e-governance.

But, crucially, vision and leadership are needed. In 2019 we saw public figures on two continents take this on in two different ways. In the USA Alexandria Ocasio-Cortez, a Democratic Congresswoman for New York, and Ed Markey, a Democratic Senator from Massachusetts, introduced a Green New Deal to kick-start a new type of US growth based on missions that would eliminate all US carbon emissions. In Europe, Ursula von der Leyen, President of the EU Commission, announced the launch of the European Green Deal, which advocated policy initiatives aimed at making Europe climate-neutral by 2050.[15] 'This is Europe's man on the moon moment,' she declared.[16]

The Green New Deal in the USA set a clear direction for its mission and established targeted, measurable and timebound goals. The resolution Senator Markey and Congresswoman Ocasio-Cortez introduced into Congress called for a 'ten-year national mobilization' towards reaching goals such as 'meeting 100 per cent of the power demand in the United States through clean, renewable, and zero-emission energy sources'. The ultimate goal was to stop using fossil fuels entirely and to move away from nuclear energy.

Within the mission, the targets included 'upgrading all existing buildings' in the country for energy efficiency; working with farmers 'to eliminate pollution and greenhouse gas emissions . . . as much as is technologically feasible' (while supporting family farms and promoting 'universal access to healthy food'); overhauling transportation systems to reduce emissions – including expanding electric car-manufacturing, building 'charging stations everywhere', and expanding high-speed rail to reduce national air travel. On top of that, the mission has social goals, including a guaranteed job with a family-sustaining wage, adequate family and medical leave, paid vacations and retirement security' and 'high-quality health care' for all Americans.[17]

Similarly, the European Green Deal set a bold, inspirational mission that imparted a guiding direction to the EU economy. Its ambition was to transform a high-carbon economy to a low-carbon one while maintaining living standards, raising quality of life and improving the natural environment. It provided fifty specific policy measures and established its intention to meet the goals of the 2016 Paris Climate Agreement. A principal objective of the European Green Deal, in making Europe climate-neutral, is to help slow down global warming and mitigate its effects. The plan envisages increasing the EU's 2030 target for net emission reductions from 40 per cent to at least 50 per cent. At the same time, the Green Deal will be Europe's growth strategy, creating jobs and improving the quality of life. This will involve cutting emissions across many sectors, from transport to taxation, food to farming, industry to agriculture. Preserving biodiversity is an important objective too. The intention is that this huge effort will catalyse enormous investment.

The Sustainable Europe Investment Plan, announced on 14 January 2020, aims to mobilize at least €1 trillion of sustainability-related investments over the next decade.[18] About half of this is to come from the EU budget, another €114 billion from national governments and €279 billion from private-sector investment supported by loan guarantees from the European Investment Bank. Another part of the plan is a Just Transition Mechanism (fund) under which €100 billion will be raised, with leverage from the European Investment Bank and private money, to help countries – especially some in eastern Europe, which depend more on fossil fuels such as a coal – to make the transition.

Such bold policies need a clear framing, along with mandatory changes to the status quo. For example, for the European Green Deal to succeed, governments need to redesign financial instruments broadly. This includes directing public banks, such as the European Investment Bank, or national banks such as the KfW in Germany, towards fuelling funds for green projects; getting the central bank to use financial regulation to reward green banking; using structural funds (which support economic development in all member states) to foster green infrastructure rather than simple 'shovel-ready' projects; and restructuring investment funds and funds for small and mid-size enterprises to focus on rewarding the most innovative companies that provide green solutions.

Proposals for policy change are under way. Underpinning the mission, the first European climate law will render the transition to climate neutrality irreversible. Among other main measures proposed are an EU Industrial Strategy and a Circular Economy Law (to stimulate further sustainable use of materials). A carbon border mechanism for certain sectors – a tariff on products from countries with inferior environmental standards designed to comply with World Trade Organization rules – is proposed as well.

It is unclear whether the EU can mobilize funding on the scale envisaged or drum up essential political support from Europe's citizens for this mission. No other country, let alone a group of countries as big as the EU, has committed to such an undertaking. But, in consciously invoking Apollo as a

precedent for the European Green Deal, Ms von der Leyen
sought to concentrate attention on the outcome rather than the
scale of the challenge and enlist the *spirit* of Apollo to steer
Europe in the twenty-first century.

In addition, a green transition will not happen without the
revolution this book is advocating in how governments operate and how the relationships between public and private
organizations are structured. For too long, governments have
over-invested in carbon and under-invested in renewable
energy sources. Mainstream economic prescriptions of simply
solving climate change with a carbon tax and some R&D subsidies (to let markets find the optimal pathway), combined
with political economic impediments to carbon taxes, have left
us with negligent carbon tax systems and a worryingly slow
green transition. The political-economic constraints are not
solely to blame here. Economists have failed to realize and set
out the reasoning for transformative public investment and re-
regulation that accomplish what CO_2 tax cannot on its own.
As behavioural science has shown (and the reader knows from
everyday life), real persons do not normally optimally react to
price incentives, and they tend to 'satisfice' (are satisfied)
rather than maximize profits or measures of happiness at every
step of the way.[19] This leaves a sizeable scope for clever, well-
informed regulations such as energy performance standards.
Furthermore, industrial change through radical innovation
and infrastructure investments cannot be expected to respond
mechanically to CO_2 taxes as a matter of supply and demand
in a farmer's market.[20] A few governments have created markets in which renewable energy technology – such as wind
power in Denmark and solar power in Germany – can flourish and develop through learning by doing, in order to give

them opportunities to mature and compete with fossil-based technology.

Our lethargic transition pace, globally, is a lesson in what can happen if government leaves the market to sort out problems and abstains from assuming its entrepreneurial role in society. It also flies in the face of what happened in that most transformative technological and business upheaval, the IT revolution, when government initiatives and investments were pivotal. This time, however, we need more than just initiatives from government. Neither the US nor the EU proposals can operate in a vacuum within sectors like renewable energy, de-carbonizing vehicles, or any other sector-specific initiatives. Instead, innovative transformation is required across all sectors, constituting one of the largest shifts humans have ever attempted.[21] Reducing the material content of heavy industries like steel, and introducing a circular economy for waste in sectors with a repurpose, reuse and recycle mentality will be critical. This requires changes to materials that can produce more durable clothing, changes to our nutrition, with more focus on locally sourced food, and switching to production techniques like 3D manufacturing.[22]

Markets will not find a green direction on their own, however. Governments have a fundamental role to play in providing a stable, consistent conduit for investment which ensures that regulation and innovation converge along a green trajectory that addresses climate change. Moreover, governments cannot resort to typical interventions such as tax incentives or public subsidies; these are simply not enough to fuel the change needed. Business will not invest unless it sees an opportunity for growth. Only bold investments like Roosevelt's New Deal will match the scale of the climate emergency.[23]

The Green New Deal has different dimensions at city, regional, national and international levels. Existing policies – such as those of mayors – change in critical ways when problem-solving is placed at the heart of strategy. This essentially means making goals central to how economic growth itself is viewed, bringing the *direction* of innovation – rather than only its rate – to the core of the discussion.

This is what Energiewende in Germany is trying to do. The implications are economy-wide because it involves not only renewable energy but also the carbon content in sectors such as steel. It profoundly affects policy design too, whether this be the conditions attached to loans made by KfW, the public bank, or how the fiscal stimulus is steered. Energiewende meets several of the defining criteria of a mission. First, it represents a grand challenge. Second, it has clear targets, including phasing out nuclear power in Germany by 2022, coal by 2038, and staggered targets for renewable electricity generation. Third, it is framed to stimulate research which may involve a wide range of participants, such as civil-society organizations, who are empowered to pursue public-purpose goals, and innovation across sectors, including some, like steel, that might not otherwise have done much to reduce emissions. Under Energiewende, the assistance that government provided to the steel industry included conditionalities that required it to reduce its carbon content by converting smelting gas from steel production into base chemicals using renewable energy. Fourth, the public understands Energiewende. The mission packages a complex mix of policy, investment and legislation into one simple idea – the mission – that makes it clear that the government, scientists and businesses are working to free society from dependence on nuclear power and replace it as much as possible with green, sustainable energy such as wind and solar. Fifth, Germany's well-established green movement has given the mission legitimacy: 90 per cent of citizens support Energiewende. And finally, a decisive event – the Fukushima nuclear disaster in Japan in 2011 – transformed a long-running effort into a mission, rather as Sputnik was the immediate impetus for Apollo.

Energiewende does face stiff challenges. The exit from nuclear power made Energiewende harder to implement because the quick closure of nuclear power plants increased the need for coal-powered ones. Trying to meet two goals at once – low-carbon energy and non-nuclear energy – can lead to contradictions if pursued too quickly. Germany is now among the laggards in the Powering Past Coal Alliance, a club of national and subnational governments pushing for the end of coal-fired electricity generation in OECD countries by 2030. If Germany does not significantly reduce its carbon emissions, Energiewende will fail in its main objective.

Another challenge is the equitable distribution of the costs of the transformation. Since a lot of renewable energy generation still benefits from generous tariff subsidies from the 2000s, when solar photo-voltaic energy in particular was very costly, Germans face significant surcharges for their electricity bills, rendering German electricity prices some of the highest in Europe. And since some energy-intensive industries or facilities are exempt (similar to exceptions from the European Emissions Trading system), the burden falls even more heavily on households, leading some to question whether public support for the project will falter.

All this brings us back to the point that social missions are harder to fulfil than purely technological ones because they combine political, regulatory and behavioural changes. Perhaps the most interesting aspect of the Energiewende is how it has created a new relationship between business and government. Steel was not just given a handout: it had to transform itself. This provides valuable lessons in how to set a bold new direction for the health sector, especially by transforming its relationship with the pharmaceutical industry – Big Pharma.

Mission: innovating for accessible health

A mission-oriented approach in the health sector, where services, therapies and diagnostics are crucial, is a particularly interesting concept because it allows us to look at how missions affect the way in which the public and private sectors *produce* together. That is, it moves us from policy to actual production. A mission-oriented approach to production means keeping an eye on the objective and governing the value chain to reach that objective. So in producing a vaccine, the mission objective might be that it is universally available and accessible. That will affect how the production and innovation itself is carried out and governed. It will include governance of the intellectual property rights, licensing agreements, and the types of collaborations between large pharmaceutical companies and public labs. Rethinking how to govern health innovation better is particularly relevant because health-innovation systems have long failed to address the world's greatest needs and put public health first.

Health innovation is expensive, inefficient and unsustainable, while the pharmaceutical sector itself consistently puts profits before people. Largely, this is due to incentives which encourage pharmaceutical companies to set high prices and deliver short-term returns to shareholders instead of investing in riskier, long-term research that advances critical therapies. The high prices of medicines have prevented patients from using them worldwide, or have reduced access to them, with damaging consequences for human health and well-being. This is especially problematic given the very high public spending worldwide on drug innovation. In the USA alone, the National Institutes of Health spends $40 billion a year on it and yet drug prices do not reflect that, leading some to say – an idea we have encountered before – that while the costs are socialized, the profits are privatized.[24]

A case in point: the hepatitis-C drug Sofosbuvir was the product of over ten years of research funded by the US Department of Veterans Affairs and NIH-funded research at Emory University, as well as NIH small-business innovation grants.[25] After acquiring the drug, Gilead Sciences originally marketed it in the USA at $84,000 for a twelve-week course at one pill a day. In the UK, the list price for a course of treatment was nearly £35,000 (excluding VAT).[26] These prices presented a huge barrier to access, even in wealthy countries. But by the end of 2017, Sofosbuvir-based products had generated over $50 billion in sales for Gilead.[27] And more recently, in July 2020, Gilead was charging $3,120 for its COVID-19 drug Remdesivir, which was co-developed with a $70.5 million grant from the government-funded NIH.[28]

Unfortunately, one of the reasons why the NIH itself has become less active in this area is because it scrapped the fair pricing clause in 1995.[29] And even though there are march-in rights under the Bayh–Dole Act, which allowed publicly financed research to be patented, unfortunately the NIH seems not to be interested in using them effectively. Indeed, no federal agency has ever exercised its power to license patent rights to others. In particular, the NIH has received six march-in petitions and has denied each one.[30] Interestingly, the Veterans Health Administration has been much more successful at getting good prices – highlighting again how military objectives seem to be better attuned to securing a good public–private deal.[31]

In 2018 I co-authored a report, 'The People's Prescription', that advocated a mission-oriented approach to health innovation and a realignment of health systems to create public value. I argued that a thriving health system should generate new health technologies that improve public health, while ensuring access to effective treatments for the people who need them. In the report, I proposed resurrecting the idea of an ARPA-H for health to crowd in the solutions needed for health innovation goals – similar to how DARPA had done so well for defence-related goals. Key to the proposal was using a mission-oriented approach to link the upstream investment in research for new drugs to the downstream access to health care; public investment in health would attract private-sector activity, but also structure the governance of the process in a way that met public interest tests. This would mean ensuring as far as possible that patents are not abused to create monopoly profits and that prices are kept lower to reflect the public contribution.

In 2020, when the global pandemic hit, the need for a mission-oriented approach to health innovation became ever more urgent. Prior to the 73rd World Health Assembly, I joined over 140 public-health figures – including fifty former world leaders – in a call to ensure that a 'people's vaccine' would be universally available to anyone across the world. The mission here was to develop and produce a COVID-19 vaccine that was affordable and globally accessible – and left no one behind.

Fortunately, researchers from universities and companies across the globe started racing to develop a vaccine as soon as the virus was identified. This mobilization was made possible only through substantial public investment, including by the NIH and the Coalition for Epidemic Preparedness Innovations, a publicly funded non-profit organization created after the West African Ebola epidemic to research and develop vaccines for deployment in outbreaks. The Biomedical Advanced Research and Development Authority, part of the US Department of Health and Human Services, also invested substantially in deals with US companies, such as Johnson & Johnson ($450 million) and Moderna ($483 million). But funding is not enough. What is needed is governance of the process in the public interest. In the UK, despite significant public funding towards a vaccine – going mainly towards twenty-five university-based projects – there are no safeguards in place to ensure that publicly funded products will be affordable and available to everyone who needs them, though the University of Oxford has made statements close to that effect. Unless such conditions are written into contracts, experience shows it does not happen.

Indeed, investing billions of dollars in R&D was, and is, just the first step in health innovation. Whether the goal is to develop a COVID-19 vaccine, an advanced treatment for cancer or an affordable medication for diabetes, governments have to radically transform the governance, structures and incentives of the health innovation model to meet the needs of patients and public health. For example, governments need to provide clear and transparent rules of engagement along the entire innovation chain. Public-health-interest goals and metrics have to govern innovation end to end, from R&D to public access to treatment. Urgent public-health needs must take top priority.

In addition, governments should steer the innovation ecosystem to use collective intelligence and innovation for public-health impact. Scientific and medical innovation thrives and progress is made when knowledge is exchanged openly, building upon shared successes and failures. But proprietary science does not follow that logic: it promotes secretive competition, prioritizes crossing regulatory finishing lines in wealthy countries over wide availability and public-health impact globally, and erects barriers to technological diffusion. While voluntary technology pools can be helpful, they risk being ineffective as long as commercial companies are allowed to retain control over critical technologies and data – even when these were generated with public investment.

The public sector, as a critical investor and participant in developing crucial technologies from vaccines, therapeutics and diagnostics, should govern the drug innovation process more like a market shaper: steering innovation, getting fair prices, ensuring that patents and competition work as intended and safeguarding medicine supply. At a global level, this requires governments to join efforts to impose firm rules regarding intellectual property, pricing and manufacturing. In the case of COVID-19, the process must also be governed in ways that value collaboration and solidarity between countries – not competition – both for R&D and for the availability and distribution of products.

Again, conditionalities are key because they can ensure that public investment is structured less like a handout and more like a market shaper, driven by public objectives. The pricing of the drugs and vaccines should reflect the substantial public contribution to their R&D, based on the real costs of research, development, manufacturing and supply. Beyond statements of principle and generic pledges, there should be concrete stipulations to make crucial vaccines – such as those for COVID-19 – free at the point of use in all health-care systems. As needed, compulsory licensing should be considered to allow countries to make the best use of the available knowledge that emerges from research.

Countries need domestic manufacturing capabilities for producing drugs and vaccines, otherwise there is no guarantee that they will have enough during emergencies as every country prioritizes access for its own population. For this, investments may be needed in a range of assets and technologies. To overcome the technological and financial risks involved, collective, public-interest-driven financing is needed at national and international levels, such as from state and regional development banks, the World Bank and philanthropy. It is also crucial to create collective procurement mechanisms and ensure fair allocation and equitable access worldwide to treatments and vaccines. In any scenario, we must prevent countries from monopolizing the global supply or excluding demand from poorer countries.

It is also interesting to think of an ambitious mission map in the area of health. Building again on the concept of healthy ageing, Figure 11 presents a mission map from my EC report on missions which looks at the kind of inter-sectoral relationships – from AI to social services – that would be

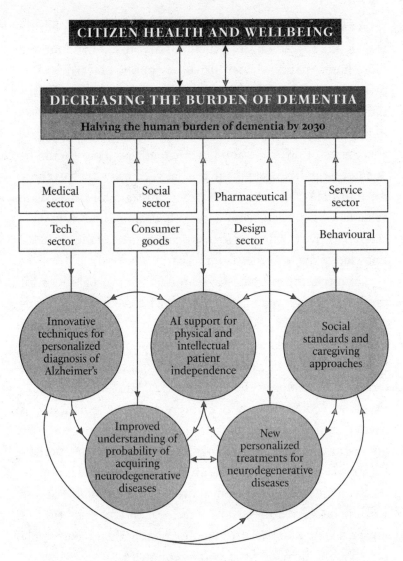

Figure 11: A mission map for 'Dementia'

involved in halving the burden of dementia by 2030. It is clear that the deeply social element of the mission requires as much attention to the behavioural, regulatory and political as to the technological. Given the link between health and inequality, most health missions are impossible to solve without tackling the social and economic factors that lie at the source of inequality. These factors are what Michael Marmot calls the 'social determinants of health'.[32] It is interesting to consider creating missions that explicitly tackle inequality. In many cities it is well known that as one moves away from the centre, life expectancy drops. For example, data shows that there is a twenty-year difference in life expectancy between people born in the centre of London near Oxford Circus and those born in east London, close to some stations on the Docklands Light Railway.[33] Similarly in the USA, in some cities like New Orleans which are plagued by high rates of poverty, crime and inequality, a difference of just a mile takes twenty years off an expected lifespan.[34] A mission could thus choose to be as specific as to even out that difference and test progress literally along the London Tube map or the NYC subway!

The next mission also looks at the deep inequalities in another field where politics meets technology.

Mission: narrowing the digital divide

In today's world, the capability to work with data and digital technology comes close to being a human right, as Sir Tim Berners-Lee, the founder of the internet, has argued.[35] Without it, there are no opportunities related to what the knowledge economy and digital connectivity provide. While technology is theoretically available for all, in actuality it is not. And the COVID-19-induced lockdown of 2020 actually widened and entrenched the digital divide, as students had unequal access to the technology needed for at-home schooling; many were stuck without broadband or enough computers, tablets or phones for learning; many also did not have the space or home environment to access online schooling resources safely, quietly and consistently. A mission for the future could target this problem and make technology more democratically available.

The digital divide is a global problem. In the USA, for example, 21 million people lack internet access, and only two-thirds of Americans have a home broadband connection.[36] The 'homework gap' – the lack of reliable internet connection to do homework – is even more pronounced among black, Hispanic and lower-income families. In the UK, 7 per cent of households have no access to the internet.[37] In 2018, 12 per cent of those aged between eleven and eighteen (700,000 young people) reported having no internet access at home from a computer or tablet, while a further 60,000 reported having no home internet access at all.[38] Of those in this age group, 68 per cent who did have home internet access reported that they would find it difficult to complete schoolwork without it. In total, 3.7 billion people around the world – half the global population – do not have internet access.[39]

To bring a mission-oriented approach to this problem, it is important to have a clear goal in mind. That goal can be used to drive innovation, aided by procurement or prize schemes that nurture creativity and allow a scaling-up process for organizations that are willing and able to experiment.

It is also important, however, to remember that 'wicked' problems cannot be solved in a linear way, and there is no purely tech solution to social problems.[40] The digital divide has multiple dimensions – technological, economic, social, cognitive and political. The first dimension concerns digital infrastructure needed to access online services through alternative channels, such as wireless data plans and wired broadband and fibre services. Microsoft's Airband Initiative estimates that, in the USA, around 157 million citizens do not have access to high-speed, high-quality internet. This means that for a significant percentage of homes, students were physically and digitally excluded from access to education during the lockdown. And their parents too were of course excluded from the possibility of remote working. Another dimension of accessibility concerns the device, device literacy, and environment in which online services are accessed. The increasing penetration of wireless data means that many rely on phones and smartphones – rather than laptops or desktops – to access online services. However, access to online resources and software on a phone is limited compared to the range of services and software available on laptops and desktops. Additionally, not everyone knows how to navigate online services or has the time to learn how to do it. Not everyone has a safe and quiet home environment in which to spend time searching online programs. Not everyone can use their device independently. Not everyone reads at the same language level or in the dominant language required for navigating online learning and resource access to make full use of the internet, or even public digital services.

A further dimension is the affordability of data and internet services. As a continuous expense, many families may have to choose between internet and data plans, for which the benefits may be unclear and which require time and experience to use. Additionally, the perception and relationship among users and internet service providers, from concerns over privacy, hidden fees and data caps, can create further barriers.

These differences combine with other inequalities to create

systematic disparities in outcomes for those with and without digital resources. As more advanced technologies, such as AI, enter the market, this current divide will be compounded as those with prior skills, experience and even moderately better equipment may gain far more even than those who are included but who lack the know-how to make use of digital resources.

In this sense, the digital divide is a bundle of different inequalities which converge to produce unequal digital outcomes – not simply division in access to internet or laptops, but division in utility of internet access, division in interest, division in relevant online opportunities, division in time for use, training, quality of connection, accessibility and so on. Thus, the main innovations needed require improving diffusion, democratization, embedded online resource navigation, and training. This necessitates the co-ordination of policies that target affordable, sustainable, accessible and valuable online access and services.

It is impossible to think of one mission that will tackle this immensely complex phenomenon. But Figure 12 looks at how we might design a mission map to involve as many different sectors as possible to eliminate the digital divide. Italy, for example, is among the laggards in Europe for digitalization, languishing in twenty-fifth position of twenty-eight countries in the Digital Economy and Society Index (DESI).[41] Only four out of ten businesses use a fast or super-fast connection. As for the 74.7 per cent of households to whom the internet is available, the gap between the Centre-North and South is too wide.[42] Sectors collaborating on such a mission would include computing hardware, digital design, education, data management, artificial intelligence, banking and energy. This is similar

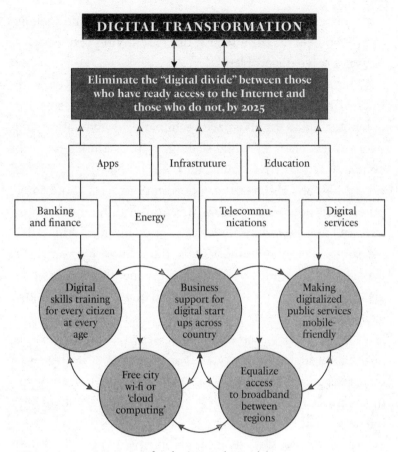

Figure 12: A mission map for the 'Digital Divide'

to the Obama administration's 2013 ConnectED goal of providing 99 per cent of American students with access to broadband in classrooms by 2018, which required co-ordination between business and the government.[43] This programme had limited success because of inequalities which it recognized but could not feasibly address – doing so would have required interaction between multiple local activities such as coding classes in youth centres and local computer access at libraries.

The concept of 'ready access to the internet' should include improved benefits, or effective use – resolving connectivity does not solve the problem.

The 1980s BBC Computer Literacy Project serves as an interesting example of how a government-led mission for computer literacy galvanized technological innovation and behavioural changes while scaling up possibilities for tech companies. The BBC launched the mission to give British households and children the opportunity to learn about computers and how to use them. It required different types of investments, including developing a computer – the BBC Micro – which would find its way into almost every British classroom.[44] It needed to satisfy basic computing needs while also being financially within the reach of all schools, not just rich ones.

The BBC Micro was the work of Acorn, a company based near Cambridge, which won the contract to make it. Procurement was used to specify the outcomes required but left much of the innovation and the 'how' to the companies involved, which were able to scale up.

The computer was advanced for its time and went through successive iterations, spawning a cottage industry of new enthusiasts who modified it to improve its performance, wrote software and games for it, and were devoted readers of magazines dedicated to the burgeoning phenomenon. Acorn later faded, but its spin-out company, ARM Holdings, is today one of the world's leading chip designers and software developers. ARM's chip architecture was pioneered in the second processor for the BBC Micro. Another legacy of Acorn is the Raspberry Pi Foundation and its ubiquitous low-cost computer, which helps educators all over the world get digital technology in the classroom. This is a good example of how mission-oriented procurement can foster a scaling-up process in business that is not the outcome of focusing on incentives for business but on public needs. And business benefits in the process.

Mission-oriented thinking cannot be based on the status quo. The mission attitude is not about picking individual sectors to support but about identifying problems that can catalyse collaboration between many different sectors. It is not about handing out money to firms because they are small or because they are in need, but structuring policies that can crowd in different solutions (projects) by multiple types of organizations. It is not about fixing markets but creating markets. It is not about de-risking but sharing risks. It is not about picking winners but picking the willing. And it is not simply about setting the 'rules of the game' but about changing the game itself so that a new direction can foster change – change towards a green transition and/or the digitalization of a population.

Given that this new language counters standard economic reasoning, the next chapter asks: what is the bold new political economy that can provide the framework for a mission-oriented economy?

PART IV: THE NEXT MISSION

Reimagining the economy and our future

6: Good Theory, Good Practice:
Seven Principles for a New Political Economy

On 16 April 2019 Greta Thunberg, the young Swedish climate activist, gave a speech to the European Parliament, calling for 'cathedral thinking' to tackle climate change:

> It is still not too late to act. It will take a far-reaching vision, it will take courage, it will take fierce, fierce determination to act now, to lay the foundations where we may not know all the details about how to shape the ceiling. In other words, it will take cathedral thinking. I ask you to please wake up and make changes required possible. To do your best is no longer good enough. We must all do the seemingly impossible.[1]

When they built the cathedrals that are among Europe's most magnificent cultural achievements, the medieval master builders took chances that would drive a modern architect out of business. Nobody knew how much it would cost to build a cathedral or how long it would take. But these were missions with a purpose – to demonstrate the glory of God through creativity – and they brought together many different sectors of society: clergy, craftsmen, nobles, rulers and ordinary people. Today, the cathedrals are still with us.

Government can build the cathedrals of mission-oriented innovation in the twenty-first century if it is recast with courage, dynamic competency, leadership, resilience and creativity.[2] But this means strengthening systems and the underlying forms of collaborations. Indeed, as is well known, many workers died building the great cathedrals. Having societal challenges drive modern innovation means embedding equity, fairness and sustainability within our systems of public health, public education, public transport. The social infrastructure that enables businesses to work and compete globally must be imagined and designed in this way from the outset.

And the relationship goes both ways. For public systems to work and be part of a healthy social fabric, we need a different type of private sector with which governments can interact. Government alone, no matter how ambitious and mission-oriented, cannot pursue a better path if it does not have a more productive relationship with business – and if business itself is not more long-term-minded and purposeful. While there are movements afoot to get business to move away from pure maximization of profits and shareholder value towards a more stakeholder-driven governance structure, so far there is little evidence that this is actually changing anything beyond the feel-good factor. Real progress will only happen when stakeholder governance and 'purpose' become central to how organizations are governed and how they interact. To address the challenges set out in this book, to change capitalism, we must therefore change the inter-relationships between government, business and civil society, especially the underlying power relationship. There are a variety of different forms of capitalism, and we have the wrong one.

Chapter 2 began with a list of the central problems in capitalism today: finance financing finance; business preoccupied with quarterly returns instead of long-run growth; global warming; and governments that are tinkering rather than steering transformative change. Chapter 3 looked at how the way in which government acts (too little too late) nests within a particular intellectual framing of what government is for: fixing markets. Chapters 4 and 5 explored the need to bring a more mission-oriented approach to public policy. This chapter argues that a more purpose-driven government and a new relationship between public and private – i.e. capitalism – requires a new political economy founded on the co-creation and shaping of markets, not just fixing them. This requires rethinking value creation as a collective endeavour. Just as existing policies and structures are informed by (problematic) theories, a mission-oriented 'practice' for policy requires a new theoretical basis driven by a new approach to market shaping and value creation.

There are, I believe, **seven key pillars** to a better political economy that can guide a mission-oriented approach. The first is about a new approach to **value** and the collective process through which it is created. We need business, government and civil society to create value together, with none being relegated to cheerleaders of the other. In this process it is necessary to define the collective creation of value and the notion of public purpose which can drive the direction of that value creation and inform how value is owned and shared.

The second is about **markets** and market shaping. Missions require a different framing for policy – not about fixing market failures but actively 'co-creating and co-shaping' markets. Shaping markets means moving our language – and our thinking – from a model in which the state's main goal is to fix and 'level' the playing field to one in which it co-creates a direction, and hence must tilt the playing field towards that direction. The latter is not about 'picking winners' but (as explained in Chapter 3) picking the willing by aligning instruments that are available to government to steer the economy in the direction that produces the kind of value we want. This means that taxation can be used to reward value creation over value extraction, and to steer value creation towards building an economy that is more inclusive and sustainable.

The third is about **organizations** and organizational change. If what is being sought is a common purpose, that requires capabilities which are about co-operation, not competition. These include the capability to take risks together and experiment; to welcome learning under conditions of uncertainty; and to use finance to serve long-term objectives rather than itself. It also includes the ability to evaluate past experiences based on a holistic view of the spillovers – both positive and negative – that occur when trying to achieve an objective. Here, it is crucial to go against the trend of governments outsourcing their capabilities and capacity and to reinvest resources into structures that foster knowledge creation, learning and creativity inside the civil service. It is impossible to co-create value without this.

The fourth is about **finance** and long-term financing. So much of today's economic discussion tends to focus on public debts and deficits. But a mission-oriented approach brings a new perspective. Getting the economy to work for societal goals, rather than society working for the economy, requires a reversal of the way budgets are thought about. We must begin with the question, 'what needs to be done?' and then move to that of how to pay for it. If structured through dynamic institutions that encourage creativity and innovation along the way, public investment can foster long-run growth.

If we can do it in wartime, why not in peacetime, when the urgency is to solve societal battles and achieve common goals?

The fifth is about **distribution** and inclusive growth. Collective value creation and market shaping make sure the creation of value and its direction gets the conditions right, so that inequality can be fought by predistribution, not only by redistribution. This means more emphasis on good jobs, collective ownership structures – including key resources such as data – rather than the usual ex-post correction via taxation. In other words, once we accept that value creation is a collective effort (value), requiring risk-taking and experimentation (capabilities), and adequate and well-structured financing (finance), the distribution of that value must reflect those principles. First, it must reward the entire set of value creators. Second, it should enable the recreation of that value by investing in the sources of creativity. Third, the financing sources must be replenished rather than extracted. Then there will be more fairness and resilience in our economic system.

The sixth is about **partnership** and stakeholder value. Emphasis on collective value creation means that how we design the collaborations between business and government matters. The notion of 'purpose' and stakeholder value is not only about changes to corporate governance but is also about the details of contracts between business and the state. The example of how NASA worked with the private sector has important lessons for modern-day partnerships, which too often are parasitic rather than symbiotic. Parasitic partnerships are ones where one organization grows at the expense of another. Symbiotic ones are where both prosper – with a common goal. How this can be done in today's markets for digital platforms, health and energy is a pressing question.

The seventh is about **participation** and co-creation. For value to be created collectively, we must foster new forms of participation in that creation process, via a revival of debate, discussion and consensus-building. For this to happen, new, decentralized forums are needed that bring together different voices and experiences, such as citizen assemblies. And if such forums and institutions are not present, they must be built. We should not forget that both Roosevelt's New Deal and the moon landing were in essence governed by the elite. The challenges of the twenty-first century will require much more interaction with citizens and communities, and indeed leadership by them. But in the first instance, a stakeholder approach to value must begin with the recognition that value is collectively created by multiple groups, including businesses, workers and local and central governments.

Together, these seven pillars can help create a new political economy – one that encourages a mission-oriented approach and builds an economy driven by public purpose and citizen engagement. Let's take a closer look at each pillar.

Value: collectively created

Missions are about bringing a high level of strategic purpose to value creation. They are an admission that growth has not only a rate but also a direction – and that direction should have purpose. Focusing investment on problem-solving requires new tools: first, a revived notion of public value and public purpose and, second, a market co-creation framework. We begin here with the first.

In 1973, J. K. Galbraith argued that the American

economy had been captured by business interests and that government had lost its way. He proposed that policy should be driven by public interest, not private interests, and that this could only happen if there was an explicit rejection of the economic orthodoxies of the past: 'With a revised view of the purpose of the economic system goes a revised view of the purpose of economics.'[3] Achieving this would require both economic and political change.

Purpose defines missions and guides how public and private actors work together, co-creating value. This collaborative process can be called the 'creation of public value'. In this context, 'public' does not mean that government is the sole actor creating value, but rather that value is collectively created by different actors and for the community as a whole, in the public interest.[4]

The notion of the public interest that needs reviving goes far back. Greek political philosophy had a strong sense of public service and the duty of the citizen to engage in public affairs. This was seen as necessary to avoid tyranny, so much so that the ancient Greeks used the term 'idiotes' (ἰδιώτης) to denote those who did not operate in the public sphere; to put it harshly, if you were only concerned with the private sector, you were an idiot. So if you were a wealthy Athenian and you didn't want to be seen as an idiot, you funded public arts like theatre festivals (as told by Xenophon, perhaps the first economist, in *Hiero*). Later the ancient Romans spoke of the 'pro bono publico', based on the ethical considerations of working for the common good, not the pursuit of profit – a term still used today in the legal sphere. A caveat: it is important to acknowledge that, despite their commitment to public purpose, the ancient Greek and Roman civilizations were deeply flawed. They were based on extreme underlying injust-ice, with slavery being common – and women having no public role (except in Rome to tend the 'vestal flame').

This ambitious notion of the public sphere is hard to recon-cile with the dominant economic framework, which rests on the assumption that people maximize their own preferences. Collective effort is missed because only individual decisions matter – with firms maximizing profits, and consumers maxi-mizing utility (a proxy for Benthamite happiness). Even wages are seen as outcomes of workers maximizing their choices between the utility earned from leisure versus that earned from work.[5] In this context, the concept of social value is limited to the aggregation of individuals (workers, managers in firms, consumers) making decisions to maximize their own economic welfare. The traditional framework also confuses price with value: only that which has a price is valuable. This means many public services that are free are not valued except through the accounting of their paid inputs (e.g. the cost of schoolteachers). Their costs are accounted for, but many of their outputs (e.g. a well-structured public-education system) are not.

As we saw in Chapter 3, public goods – such as education, basic research or clean air – are seen not as *objectives* created by the collective imagination of 'what to do', but as filling gaps where the private sector does not go. But if our economy were driven by public purpose, we would not ask, 'What gap or market failure are public goods filling?' but rather, 'What are public goods the solution to?' and 'What form must they take to benefit us the most?'. To steer our understanding of public interest, it is useful to consider public goods not as corrections of market failures but as common objectives. Common goods are the result of collective imagination, investment and pressure from social movements, from clean air to public education. Producing these well requires the right knowledge and capabilities to plan and manage them, including interactions between different interest groups. In this sense the production of common goods via public purpose needs a theory of collective value creation.

While the traditional question defining public goods is 'Is it possible to exclude those who do not pay for the good?', the key question for the broader concept of the common goods is, as the public management theorist Barry Bozeman has framed it for public-value creation: 'Have those public values endorsed by society been provided or guaranteed?'[6] Embedding those values into the production of common goods becomes essential in both physical and social infrastructure. Such questions are fundamental for how we govern twenty-first-century capitalism: how we produce health innovation (vaccine production governed by notions of collective intelligence), how we govern digital platforms (with data seen as a human right), and how we co-design a green transition where different voices imagine together a new way to live in our cities, from the future of mobility to carbon-neutral construction to experimental public spaces. Only by redirecting our economy — with notions of the common good and public value at the centre of production, distribution and consumption — can we shape and co-create the economy to produce a more inclusive and sustainable society.

Markets: shaping not fixing

The collective creation of value, which should be at the centre of a common-good approach, requires justifying policy in terms of actively creating and shaping markets, not fixing them. Market failure theory (MFT) assumes that markets are efficient and, when they fail, government should fix them. Government steps in to correct the sources of market failures such as positive externalities (where, due to the high spillovers, there is underinvestment by the private sector, requiring government to fund areas such as basic research); negative externalities (such as pollution, which might require government to impose carbon taxes); and asymmetric information (which can mean that banks don't know enough about new companies, requiring SME lending by governments).

MFT has major flaws as a theory but it has nevertheless been adopted as a guide to public policy. It uses as a benchmark perfectly competitive markets characterized by perfect information, completeness, an absence of transaction costs and frictions and so on. So, to measure real markets – that is, markets in which firms compete through innovation and which will often be oligopolistic or characterized by monopoly power (e.g. because of the presence of patents) – MFT argues that the distance from a perfectly competitive market must be ascertained. Yet empirically, perfectly competitive markets don't exist: markets are nearly *always* incomplete and imperfect.[7] Government may therefore always be able to improve upon a decentralized market outcome, regardless of whether the result of government intervention is inefficient in a Pareto-optimal sense. This does not mean that it is incorrect to tackle market failures, such as pollution, through instruments such as carbon taxes. It just means that we need a better theory of competition to serve as the benchmark. And given that innovation is central to how firms compete, the drivers of innovation and issues around its direction should be at the centre of how we think about competition, not relegated to a list of 'imperfections'. Furthermore, in economies aiming for transformational growth trajectories (e.g. in a green transition), it will be hard to simply 'fix' failures to get there.

And indeed, the examples we looked at in Chapters 4 and 5, from the moon landing to trying to tackle the SDGs, have required government doing much more than just fixing market failures. They require imagining new landscapes, not fixing existing ones, and aligning policies to inspire different actors who can spot opportunities for investment they did not see before. This is not about facilitating investment but catalysing it through the creation of new markets. This happened with the moon landing, which stimulated decades of investments in areas such as software. And it has happened more recently with the green economy: only after government led with high-risk, capital-intensive investments in green technology (e.g. early investments in solar and wind) did the private sector follow, eventually rendering the technologies more competitive.

This means that a broader view of policy can be based on market shaping, not only market fixing, which begins with the question: what sort of markets do we want? Attention needs to be paid both to the quantity of investment needed and also to its quality – and the underlying governance mechanisms. So in the health area, this would require broadening the notion of health to well-being, and investing not only in new remedies but also in new forms of preventative care and governing the intellectual property regime to deliver the outcomes desired. When patents are seen purely from a regulation angle, this perpetuates the idea that innovation occurs in the private sphere and is simply fixed in the public one. But, given the enormous public investments in creating value, patents should

Market failure	Market shaping
Market failure occurs when the market does not provide valuable goods or services. The main types of market failure are: • Externalities: the impact of a decision that affects others (positively or negatively). E.g. Pollution is a negative externality	While 'market fixing' is the reactive action taken to address an identified market failure, 'market shaping' is the proactive action taken to build a new market and associated ecosystem. It pushes technological and/or market frontiers rather than operating within existing frontiers
• Public goods: A public good is a good or service which is non-rivalrous and non-excludable. A failure occurs when consumers do not want to pay for the good, or 'free-ride' on those that do. Or when a private company does not want to invest in the good because of the inability to fully appropriate the profits	Market shaping takes a dynamic and ecosystem perspective of government spending, seeing it as investment in the growth of markets – both their rate of growth and their direction – as opposed to the correction of a failure
• Natural monopolies: these occur due to large economies of scale in production such that the cost of provision by one firm is cheaper than the cost of provision by more than one	This recognizes that markets are dynamic, complex, and result from both public and private activity/ investments

Table 3: Market failure vs. market shaping

deliver in the public interest. This means they should be weak (easy to license), narrow (not used for purely strategic reasons) and not too far upstream (so the tools for research remain in the open domain).[8]

Thus a market-shaping perspective requires goal-oriented investment on the supply side, market creation on the demand side, and governance mechanisms (e.g. of patents) to achieve inclusive, innovation-led and sustainable growth. Table 3 helps to compare and contrast a market-fixing with a more proactive market-shaping perspective.

Organizations: dynamic capabilities

To co-create value and shape markets, public and private organizations need dynamic capabilities of experimentation and learning. While the need to be a learning organization is often emphasized in the private sector, it is not so true in the public sector which has, as discussed in Chapter 3, been relegated to the role of a simple market fixer and enabler of value created by business. A more proactive, market-shaping approach requires rethinking the ways in which public organizations create and implement strategic actions (from leadership capabilities to how they engage with groups, other organizations and even individuals in society), rethinking how the civil service is developed (from training to performance assessment and promotion), and rethinking how work in public organizations is managed (from cross-sectoral teams to iterative experimentation, a process which goes through several stages, developing the concept and testing it to produce a workable innovation).[10]

In the private sector, managers are taught how to be flexible and adaptable, and there is an abundance of thinking about the capabilities private actors need because they are deemed to be value creators. These skills are at the heart of MBA courses in strategic management, organizational behaviour and decision sciences worldwide. And yet there are few models of learning and working dynamically inside government.

One of the pioneers of the new business thinking was the economist Edith Penrose,[11] who in the 1950s argued that competitiveness was about internal resources, especially the ability to learn. Building on her work, organizational theorists like David Teece, from the Haas School of Business at the University of California, Berkeley, developed the concept of the 'dynamic capabilities' of the firm, the internal capabilities to 'integrate, build, and reconfigure internal and external competences to address rapidly changing environments'.[12] This approach differed from that of Michael Porter, a renowned business scholar from Harvard Business School, who emphasized the need for firms to position themselves across their competitive environment (focusing on their suppliers, customers and competitors).[13] The emphasis on internal capabilities meant paying less attention to the external environment and more to the ability to learn, pivot, be agile and *adapt* to complex environments.

Mission-oriented thinking requires that we discover the importance of those features inside all organizations that tackle problems together, including those in the public sector. Yet because it's assumed that government is not crucial to value creation, only to market-fixing, attention has not been paid to the capabilities and skills for value creation and risk-taking within the public sector. Not surprisingly, many public organizations have concentrated on increasing the marginal efficiency of their activities rather than on more ambitious change.[14]

Dynamic capabilities help organizations develop and improve resources such as knowledge and are different from static operational capabilities, which are part of an organization's *existing* operations and resource base. Dynamic capabilities are part of the 'core competencies' needed to change short-term competitive positions that are eventually used to create longer-term competitive advantage. Learning by doing is a key element in improving an organization's fitness and developing 'absorptive capacity' – that is, the ability to understand the world around it.[15]

This is what the UK government failed to recognize in its outsourcing of the response to the COVID-19 pandemic.

By relying on consultancy firms to manage the test-and-trace system, the government has not only deprived our brilliant civil servants of an opportunity to demonstrate and develop their knowledge, but in doing so undermined the possibility of organizational learning through the crisis.

New challenges are daunting, but they are also an opportunity to augment capabilities in the public sector. Instead, all too often governments have not invested in organizational learning processes but instead over-relied on consultancy firms to manage difficult tasks. In the UK, after the Brexit referendum, spending on consultancies rose by £1.5 billion in 2018, and similarly, with the COVID-19 pandemic, £56 million was used in 2020 to outsource the test-and-trace system – hardly the kind of moonshot thinking that saw NASA, wary of capture and 'brochuremanship', invest in inhouse capabilities.

Rethinking government capabilities can benefit from the work of Richard Nelson and Sidney Winter, two economists known for their pioneering study of innovation and competition in economics, grounded in the work of the innovation scholar Joseph Schumpeter. Nelson and Winter helped economists understand why the 'black box' (so called because its explanation was limited) production function of economic theory (input and outputs) needed to be dismantled to really understand the dynamics of innovation, and especially how innovation happens in conditions of uncertainty.[16] Their work on 'evolutionary economics' posits that economic agents adapt to uncertainty by setting routines and rules of thumb, and that those evolve over time via experimentation and learning – and only some survive the competitive selection process. Their work is built on the thinking of Herbert Simon, a cognitive psychologist, who argued that economic actors are 'bounded' in their rationality, so do not operate by maximizing but by 'satisficing': they content themselves with being satisfied, not necessarily to the highest degree. Indeed, if businesses were constantly changing what they were doing to maximize profits (a function of costs and prices), they would never learn – there would be no *learning by doing* since what was being done would be constantly changing, as prices and costs change. In other words, a theory of innovation needs to be nested in a theory of learning, experimentation and adaptation to uncertainty.

In Chapter 4 we looked at fundamental attributes and principles that laid the foundation for government's ability to lead a mission to the moon. Following on from those, five capabilities are, I believe, central to modern bureaucracies' ability to manage complex and 'wicked' problems:[17]

Leadership and engagement: A market co-creating role requires government to have capabilities for leadership and engagement; missions can all too quickly become either just fashionable labels on 'business-as-usual' practices or over-rigid top-down planning exercises. Thus, capabilities to engage with a wide set of social actors and display leadership through bold vision are vital in times with high 'democratic deficit' in many developed countries. Some of the grand challenges contest the way of life as we know it (e.g. suburbanization accompanied by congested transportation systems). Having capabilities to encourage bottom-up engagement means that there is a capacity both to set mission but also leave enough space for contestation and adaptability.[18]

Co-ordination: The ability to find coherent policy mixes (instruments and funding) and capabilities of co-ordination are fundamental to the success of today's mission-oriented policies. As these are not just about technological solutions but include strong socio-political aspects, experimentation capabilities matter more than before. Working across departmental silos is crucial.

Administration: Administrative capabilities need especially to benefit from a diversity of expertise and skills, from engineering to human-centric design. And the management of missions requires new organizational forms to mix unrelated knowledge areas (e.g. in urban mobility and planning, lifestyles matter as much as new energy storage systems) and organizational fluidity (e.g. cross-departmental teams).[19]

Risk-taking and experimentation. A key capability needed by governments is to take risks, welcome uncertainty and learn through trial and error. Learning is, by definition, a dynamic skill. It takes time, and therefore means embedding patience into the system. Static measures of efficiency – that is, output per input – do not capture this dynamism. And many of the supposed reforms undertaken to achieve efficiency have outsourced key capabilities for learning and knowledge creation and in the process hollowed out public organizations, reducing their ability to learn and to adapt to uncertainty.

Dynamic evaluation. Equally important are evaluation capabilities that do not rely only on market-failure-based approaches (e.g. cost–benefit analysis) but can integrate experimentation and put citizens at the centre of the process (e.g. citizen as user) to make sure the system is working for them.[20] Mission-oriented policies have a clear metric: was the mission achieved? But along the way, other things happen; indeed, an attribute of innovation is that while searching for one thing another thing is discovered. Thus, metrics need to capture the dynamic spillovers that are created, as discussed in Chapter 4. That requires paying less attention to static CBA and more to dynamic feedback effects. While CBA and net present value calculations rest on static assumptions about market prices and costs, strategic mission-oriented investments often lead to a shifting of the technology frontier (to use the most advanced technology), which can have ripple effects across the economy – so nothing is held equal. Even an investment like that which led to Concorde should be measured not only by whether the plane was flying but also by the effects which the investment had across multiple sectors. Thus, new evaluation indicators are needed to capture the economy-wide benefits of such policies, including dynamic spillovers and additionality. Additionality means the way in which policies make things happen that would not have happened anyway. This is key, as so many policies focused on incentives, just about reducing the costs of business investment that would have happened in any case. What really drives business investment are expectations of where future opportunities lie. So evaluating the degree to which policies change those expectations is key. In this sense, it is essential to move beyond CBA and allocative efficiency to embrace a more dynamic notion of efficiency.[21] Table 4 builds on Tables 3's distinction between market fixing and market shaping, concentrating on the different assumptions which inform the remit and evaluation of public investments in each.

	Market fixing	Market shaping
Justification for the role of government	Market or co-ordination failures: • Public goods • Negative externalities • Imperfect competition/information	All markets and institutions are co-created by public, private and third sectors. Role of government is to ensure markets support public purpose, by involving users in co-creation of policy
Business case appraisal	Ex-ante cost-benefit analysis (CBA) – allocative efficiency assuming static general relationships, prices etc.	Focused on systematic change to achieve mission-dynamic efficiency (including innovation, spillover effects and systematic change)
Underlying assumptions	Possible to estimate reliable future value using discounting. System is characterized by equilibrium behaviour	Future is uncertain because of potential for novelty and structural change; system is characterized by complex behaviour
Evaluation	Focus on whether specific policy solves market failure and whether government failure avoided (Parento efficient)	Ongoing and reflexive evaluation of whether system is moving in direction of mission via achievement of intermediate milestones and user engagement. Focus on portfolio of policies and interventions, and their interaction
Approach to risk	Highly risk averse; opitimum bias assumed	Failure is accepted and encouraged as a learning device

Table 4: Dynamic evaluation of public investment: a market-shaping view

Finance: outcomes-based budgeting

Missions require long-term thinking and patient finance. Like any other undertaking, missions must be paid for. As was discussed in Chapter 4, Kennedy was clear that the Apollo project would cost a lot of money – and it did. And while he and NASA had to constantly defend the use of the budget, in the end the pressure and urgency to 'beat the Russians' made the money come through. Indeed, the urgency to win is why money is always available for wartime missions – whether in the world wars or Vietnam or Iraq. Money seems to be created for this purpose.

There is no reason why a 'whatever it takes' mentality cannot be used for social problems. Yet the conventional approach is to assume that budgets are fixed, and so if money is spent in one area, it will be at the expense of another area. For example, if you want new energy infrastructure, you can't have new hospitals as well. But what if budgets were based on *outcomes* to be reached, as they were for the moon landing and in wars? What if the first question is not 'Can we afford it?' but 'What do we really want to do? And how do we create the resources required to realize the mission?'

The idea may seem strange and new, but it's not. It's how things actually work from the technical point of view. In March 2005 Paul Ryan, a Republican Senator from Wisconsin, questioned Alan Greenspan, then Chair of the US Federal Reserve Board, in a Senate hearing on the US pension system. He asked whether a pay-as-you-go system was affordable and whether there would be a cash-flow problem. Greenspan answered clearly: 'There is nothing to prevent the government from creating as much money as it wants and paying it to somebody. The question is, how do you set up a system which assures the real assets are created which those benefits are employed to purchase. So, it's not a question of security. It's a question of the structure of a financial system which assures that the real resources are created for retirement as distinct from the cash.' In other words, the key question is whether the economy has the productive capacity to make good use of the money that is created and placed in private hands.[22]

Missions give spending and investment precisely that directionality to expand the productive capacity in a desired direction. That direction is what should be examined and debated, not whether there is enough money to do it. The reply is usually: but what if government continues indefinitely to increase its stock of borrowing to meet its social security commitments? We can't go on spending more than we earn. Someday there will be terrible debt reckoning. There's no magic money tree.

But that logic confuses household finances with those of a government. It is indeed true that a household can't go on spending more than it earns for long without selling possessions, securing more income or cutting expenditure. But governments don't work that way. The reason is simple: they print the money, they have a sovereign currency. When government decides to spend money on social security, defence or highways, the central bank — whether that's the European Central Bank, the Bank of England or the Federal Reserve — essentially makes the money available. It does not bounce the government's cheques. Because a central bank can issue pounds or dollars, it simply keeps the score much as the scorekeeper in a football game can count without limit how many goals each side bangs into the net. The debt keeps accumulating, and interest costs will rise, but so long as people want to hold the country's currency and — Greenspan's point — the money created is invested productively, the debt can be carried without defaulting.

Recently, economists such as Stephanie Kelton, who belong to the economic school called modern money theory (MMT), have been trying to get governments to realize that the idea that they have to come up with money before they can spend is reverse logic. In reality, spending itself creates money.[23] The thinking builds on the work of Hyman Minsky, who wrote about the theory of money beyond the notion that it simply oils the wheels of commerce. Here's how it works when applied to governments that are issuing their own currency, and are thus the *monopoly issuers* of that currency. The process logically starts with government spending/investing money. This is obvious, given that citizens cannot get their hands on money that is issued by government if the government had not spent or lent it into existence in the first place. Every time the government spends money, it taxes some of it back afterwards. If the government spends £10 and taxes £4, it can be said to be in deficit by £6. But that £6 is also in the hands of people and businesses. They are £6 better off. The other side of a government deficit is a private surplus. In other words, the government's and the private sector's balance sheets must be mirror images of each other (it is more complicated when we include exports and imports, but we do not need to do that for this discussion). A government deficit 'blows' British pounds onto balance sheets, while a government surplus 'sucks' pounds off balance sheets. A sustained fiscal surplus means constant sucking, which means that the private sector is losing financial assets, as maturing bonds are not reissued. Thus, fiscal surpluses weaken private-sector balance sheets.

It is useful to consider how budgeting actually works. A government department must first decide what it wants to do – and hence what missions are worth pursuing. Then it must persuade Parliament or Congress to accept a line in the national budget dedicated to that mission. If Parliament or Congress is persuaded, the relevant agency appropriates the budget and gets on with the job. Reducing or removing a budget in one department does not necessarily mean that more money is created for another department. Cutting NASA's funding in the 1960s, for example, would not automatically have released more cash for the US Agency for International Development or Department of Health and Human Services.

What happens to the money government is spending when it gets into private hands? Much of it is invested in government bonds. Unlike mere pounds or dollars, these bonds pay interest at a guaranteed rate. They are also highly liquid. In fact, government bonds are the lynchpin of the financial system and the core of many portfolios: pensioners who complain about government profligacy are probably living off income partly derived from government bonds. The national debt, which so exercises many politicians and citizens, is actually the historical accumulation of money spent by government, not taxed back, and now a privately held asset.[24] Government red ink equals private-sector black ink.

In 2020, events around COVID-19 took this theory of money creation in an unexpected direction. In March that year, the US Congress was terrified that the coronavirus pandemic would cause an economic disaster to rival the Great Depression of the 1930s. It voted for a $2 trillion rescue package. And the Governor of the Bank of England, Andrew Bailey, revealed in June 2020 that the bank had bought £200 billion worth of UK government bonds in April because there was a danger that the government could become insolvent.[25] What set the US package apart, however, was not just its size. It was the absence of an offset. When Congress agrees to spending measures, it usually sends two instructions to the Federal Reserve. One is to add dollars by computer to the credit of the US Treasury, which distributes the dollars to be spent as agreed. The other is to subtract dollars in the form of agreed taxes. In the case of the $2 trillion package, however, the instruction was only to *add* dollars. Money was indeed created out of thin air.

While there are many controversies around who actually

benefits from the relief packages, with many arguing that too large a part of the funds went to bailouts for companies rather than to proper relief for workers and citizens, the exceptional size of the package raises fundamental questions about the choices we have during more normal times. On an average night in the 2000s, about 500,000 Americans are homeless. Why had Congress never been able to find money to house them? Or to feed millions of hungry children? Or to provide clean drinking water for the residents of Flint, Michigan and other places who have been plagued for years by polluted water supplies? Why, for that matter, given the pandemic, had Congress not ensured that the USA had a health-care system that adequately covered the entire population? There are, of course, political answers to these questions – answers often to be found in the power of lobby groups. But the choices are not principally financial because, as we have seen, sovereign governments can (and do) create money.[26] What convinces them to consider something urgent enough to be acted on without asking the false question: is there enough money in the piggy bank to do it?

Of course, this does not mean that money can or should be created without limit. The real question is, what is the limit? The answer is inflation and how much of it can be tolerated. The key issue, as Greenspan explained, is how productive the spending is. Social security can look like a Ponzi scheme because the number of workers per social security retiree in the USA has fallen from 16:1 in 1950 to about 2:1 today. But if those two workers are much more productive than their sixteen grandparents were in 1950, the pensions will go on being paid. Similarly, as long as additional spending fuelled by government money creation does not bump up against the real resources of the economy – supply of workers, factories, machines, raw materials, technical know-how and so on – the risk of excessive inflation is low.[27] And of course that supply is not static – it can grow. Investments in physical capital (machinery, factories) and the underlying organizational and technological innovation can expand capacity.

There is no reason why investing and spending will cause inflation as long as the economy has room to grow and is not running at full capacity (human and physical). This means that making investments which expand the economy due to their strategic nature (patient, long-run and mission-oriented) – as opposed to investments that just pour money into a static economy – rarely cause inflation. They expand the pie rather than increase the money in an existing pie.

The inflation of the 1970s, which came alongside high unemployment (stagflation), was not caused by capacity constraints. It was a supply-side phenomenon, with contributing factors including oil price shocks, tight money and wage-indexation. And it happened not only in the USA, but over much of the developed world. The inflation experienced during the Weimer Republic in 1921–3 is another supply-side story. The French and Belgian armies retaliated after the German default in 1922 and took over the Ruhr, Germany's mining and manufacturing heartland. The Germans, in turn, stopped work and production ground to a halt. The Germans kept paying the workers in local currency even though only limited production was possible, so nominal demand quickly started to rise relative to real output, which was grinding to a halt. It is this kind of dynamic that can cause inflation. But this was not a normal situation in which a sovereign government was trying to finance the non-government sector's desire to save and keep employment and output levels high.

Some argue that inflation can also be caused by cancelling debt. But this too is wrong. A model of the economic impact of student debt cancellation in the USA, using conventional macro models, found that it would push up inflation by only 0.3 percentage points (at the peak).[28] Another model done by Moody's found the effect even smaller, adding a trivial 0.09 percentage points to the inflation rate.

When public investment is done strategically, with a system of organizations in the public sphere investing in long-run growth areas – including the key factors that increase productivity (education, research, science–industry linkages, worker training, patient finance etc.) – it crowds in private-sector investment. By expanding capacity, it will not cause inflation. Keeping citizens healthy with a holistic approach to their well-being (mental, physical and social) also expands capacity.

Long-run, vision-oriented public investments also have a greater possibility of creating a significant multiplier effect; that is, adding to GDP more than the total amount of investment. This is due to the way in which missions can create intersectoral effects and is a reason to think more strategically about public investments.[29]

An outcomes-based economy is one where finance serves the economy, rather than the economy serving finance. The Jesuits did well when they agreed that the money box for their missions could only be opened with two keys: one held by the *rettore* (the visionary), and one by the *procuratore* (the accountant). The vision and release of funds have to go hand in hand.[30]

Distribution: sharing risks and rewards

Discussions about how to decrease inequality are rarely linked to ones about innovation and wealth creation. The former tend to be more interested in social inclusion and reforms of the welfare state, and the latter in productivity and innovation policies around entrepreneurship. Yet a market-shaping perspective on collective value creation needs to bring together these communities and related discussions. It asks: if wealth is created socially, what are the tools to make sure wealth is also distributed socially – both for considerations of equity but also for fairness in effort and skin in the game?

This is what *predistribution* is about.[31] While *redistribution* advocates addressing inequality by redistributing income after it's created, such as through taxes or benefits, predistribution aims to prevent inequality *ex ante*. They are both needed to achieve equitable outcomes, but predistribution focuses more on getting the conditions right in the first place, so less redistribution is needed to make corrections afterwards. The idea is that if value is created collectively through societal effort, all actors should be getting their fair share in proportion to their risk-taking, input and creativity. Identifying these actors and their interactions also raises the question of how benefits are distributed among them. A predistribution approach creates structures that lead to fairer outcomes in the economy, such as contracts which ensure that the public and private sectors share the risks and rewards of value creation.

Given the immense investments involved in a mission, along with the risks of failure, it makes sense for government to consider ways to share the benefits of that investment with the widest number of citizens. Indeed, because innovation is inherently uncertain and investments have no guaranteed return, strengthening public control over rewards is a necessary condition for legitimizing government's role in creating and shaping markets. If public agencies are to absorb high technological and market risks, there is a valid expectation that the fruits of successful public finance will serve taxpayers and provide a rationale for socializing the financial rewards achieved.[32]

This can be done in various ways. One is to do it directly through a public-wealth fund, built up by the returns from government-funded activity or through equity stakes in companies benefiting from public investments. The returns from such activities can be distributed through a citizen's dividend, in essence rewarding collective value creators with a share of the wealth they created. Such public wealth could be derived from natural resources or through processes that have engaged massive collective efforts, such as the innovations that have led to path-breaking technologies like the internet or artificial intelligence.[33] This runs counter to the more commonplace situation where government investment leads to socialization of risks but privatization of rewards. That happens especially in times of crisis when companies are bailed out, but then if they recover the profits go private. But it has also happened as a normal outcome of innovation financing.

By allowing government to retain equity stakes in companies that have benefited from public investments, wealth funds can be replenished. When Tesla (discussed in Chapter 3) benefited from a $465 million guaranteed loan, strangely the US Department of Energy negotiated backwards, apparently asking that the government retain 3 million shares only if the loan was *not* paid back! Afterwards, the price per share increased nearly tenfold. Had the US government retained an equity stake in that investment in 2009, it would have earned more than enough by 2013 (when the loan was paid back) to cover the Solyndra loss and fund the next round of investments – which was the thinking that a venture capitalist would have had. But such logic requires changing the narrative to one of value creation – away from government as a lender of last resort to being an investor of first resort, thus allowing taxpayers to get a share of the value they contribute to. This is less relevant for upstream investments in basic research, the benefits of which do come back to society through knowledge spillovers. But the downstream investments going directly to companies – including during periods of bailouts – are high-risk and should indeed benefit the (collective) risk-takers in that process.

The prospect of government owning a stake in a private corporation will be anathema to many parts of the capitalist world. But, given that governments are already investing in the private sector, they may as well earn a return on those investments (something even fiscal conservatives might find attractive). Government need not hold a controlling stake, but it could hold equity in the form of preferred stocks that get priority in receiving dividends or have a 'golden share' that gives it veto rights in certain circumstances such as takeovers. The returns could be used to fund future innovation. When governments provided massive bailouts during the COVID-19 crisis, even the *Financial Times* advocated that they should retain equity stakes, so they could cover the debt that was being accrued.[34]

A more indirect way to achieve a proper public return for

public investment is to link public investments or subsidies that benefit the private sector with strong conditions that foster inclusive and sustainable growth (partly addressed in Chapter 5). Conditions can be attached to loan guarantees and bailouts that governments give to business. Such conditions can require companies which receive public funds to reinvest profits back into areas that benefit society: carbon-reduction worker training and investments in R&D. Conditions could also limit the amount of value that is extracted via share buy-backs, as US Senator Elizabeth Warren argued should be the case with bailouts during the COVID-19 epidemic. Indeed, for its COVID-related recovery funds, Denmark was clear that those companies using tax havens would not have access to government help. Other conditions might be to make sure that medicines that receive public investment – indeed, most medicines – are affordably priced.[35]

These questions about sharing rewards are all about linking value creation with value distribution. The answer to the question 'Who gets what and why?' will also determine how the relevant system reproduces itself. The eighteenth-century economists known as the Physiocrats worried that some classes in society (the merchants and the landlords) were siphoning too much value out of the system, so that the true source of value creation – agriculture – would be hurt.[36] This is why they called the merchants and the landlords, who they believed extracted more value than they created, *the sterile class*.

Keynes also believed it was critical to connect value creation with its distribution through the *socialization of investment*, a concept he briefly wrote about in the concluding chapter of his 1936 magnum opus *The General Theory of Employment,*

Interest and Money. There, he identified three major tasks to be undertaken in order to save capitalism from its own demise: 'parting with liquidity', 'euthanizing the rentiers' and 'socializing investment'. He connected the three concepts because of their role in preserving 'effective demand' – spending by consumers, investment by firms and the government. If value is siphoned out, then these sources of growth will be hurt. Socialization of investment is an important concept because it highlights that it is not only important to think of aggregate investment and demand, but also the *form* of that investment. Keynes was interested in mutual companies and co-operatives because they shared risks and rewards; that is, they reinvested profits back into the company for long-term growth and income was distributed between the collective sets of owners.

Partnership: purpose and stakeholder value

The thinking above – about how to ensure equitable relationships and a public return for a public investment – will help to build more mutualistic and symbiotic value-creating ecosystems. While the term 'public–private partnership' is often used, we need to think more about how to develop true partnerships that benefit all. As was discussed in Chapter 4, getting to the moon required an enormous effort by both public and private actors. NASA thought long and hard about how to ensure that the contracts between itself and the private providers were fair, embedded the right incentives, and did not result in capture.

In recent years the concept of 'stakeholder value' has been revived to explore ways to counter the short-termism that accompanies focusing only on shareholder value. The latter has led to companies focusing on simply maximizing profits, which then are distributed to shareholders through dividend pay-outs and through practices such as share buybacks that increase stock prices. A stakeholder view needs instead to reward all stakeholders, not only shareholders: workers, the communities and the environment. This concept recognizes that value is collectively created – so the rewards must be distributed equitably – and most of all that companies need to focus on the long term, not the short term. Long-term thinking by definition is linked to thinking about all the sources of wealth creation that must be financed, as well as the different voices that should contribute to decisions about what to finance. Under stakeholder corporate governance, companies are controlled, directly or indirectly, by shareholders and the wider group of stakeholders. For example, in Scandinavia workers' trade unions have representatives on the boards of companies and have a say on the types of investments made in their future, as well as on issues around remuneration.

Stakeholder value brings purpose to the interaction of different economic actors and the creation of value in support of a common good. The value created is reinvested back into a wider group of actors, including the community.[37] Critical to a mission-oriented view of stakeholder governance is the focus on relationships – for example, those between the public and private actors. In this sense, the commitment not to use tax havens, to invest in worker training or to lower carbon commitments in exchange for access to publicly financed technology or subsidies can become the norm. This type of conditionality could be used both in bad times – such as conditions on which to receive bailouts – but also in good times in order to receive contracts for building better health systems and renewable energy.

But fundamentally, stakeholder value needs to be seen as a way to produce differently. A perfect example is vaccine production (as discussed in Chapter 5). The public sector needs to govern vaccines as a market shaper: steering innovation, getting fair prices, ensuring that patents and competition work as intended and safeguard supply. Patent pools (agreements between patent holders to cross-license patents to each other) can enable research institutions, academia, companies and other key players across different countries collectively to govern and utilize intellectual properties to co-shape, co-create and scale up technological solutions and ensure affordable and universal access for all. The patent pools advocated by the World Health Organization to foster 'collective intelligence' could be a mechanism of solidarity, driving a common desire for collective action at one of the most sensitive inflection points in public health.[38] This would also help patents to promote productive rather than unproductive entrepreneurship.[39]

Another interesting example is modern-day space exploration. Historically, state actors such as NASA in the USA or the European Space Agency are the ones who have made the high-risk, capital-intensive investments. Today there are many private actors in space, from Elon Musk with SpaceX to Richard Branson with Virgin Galactic. These private actors are standing on the shoulders of giants that invested in the most high-risk stage of space exploration. What is the right way to share the rewards that result from this partnership? Elon Musk has reportedly received $4.9 billion in public subsidies for his three companies, including SpaceX.[40] This

support is not part of the narrative of his entrepreneurial success story, and it is also not reflected in concrete contracts;
there is no sharing of the rewards of money made on the backs
of taxpayers.

With the private sector increasingly involved in space, it is
critical that the public sector backing this involvement retains
the confidence needed to ensure that public objectives are met.
In recent years, astronauts have complained there is too much
'clutter' in space. For example, Musk's SpaceX has sent thousands of satellites into space; ultimately, it plans to launch
12,000 satellites to create a space-based internet. These satellites, called CubeSats, are very small and hence much cheaper
to produce. They are one of the reasons it has become so
much easier for private companies to enter space. But this is
also why space is now cluttered, making it harder to see the
sky at night from earth and increasing the danger of col-
lisions.[41] All of this points to the need to make sure that the
public–private partnership is a true one and not simply a
crowded one – literally.

Another key area is digital platforms. How to govern
digital platforms in a way that fosters value creation for the
majority of citizens, rather than private profits for the few, is
a major issue today. The large technology companies have
amassed record profits from the use of technologies such as
the internet and artificial intelligence. These 'big tech' companies, sometimes called FAANG (Facebook, Apple,
Amazon, Netflix and Google), have benefited from network
economies which give early movers an advantage since consumers want to be on the same platform as others they can
interact with. This, mixed with vast advertising revenues, has
created a platform economy characterized by strong and

increasing returns to scale, in which companies such as Amazon and Google hold enormous market power. The problem is they have increasingly used this power to extract what I have called 'algorithmic rents' in a modern capitalist system that looks more like 'digital feudalism'[42] – the ability to use algorithms to manipulate what people see and what they want. As the social psychologist Shoshana Zuboff has argued, we think we are lucky because we can search Google for 'free', but actually Google is searching us for free, and making a killing in the process.[43] The abilities of these large companies to sell our personal data, and manipulate searches so that their advertising revenues increase, are big problems which competition authorities have to grapple with, along with the problems associated with tax avoidance (the common strategy of shifting the source of profits to minimize tax owed). The fact that much of the 'tech' underlying 'Big Tech' is a product of public investment creates an even stronger case that publicly funded technology must serve the public interest. This requires regulation from a market-shaping perspective, and the need to find ways for governments to reward value creation, not value extraction.

Defending the underlying public interest can be framed in terms of the approach to the 'commons' – such as the data commons. Previous work on governing the commons, such as that of the economist Elinor Ostrom, stressed how to structure ways in which to share a common good to make sure it is also reproduced over time, rather than being destroyed by individual self-interest. Ostrom's critical work looked at how areas that are communally owned (for example, ocean fisheries) can be mismanaged because they are overly used (catching too many fish relative to stocks) and the common area is destroyed, providing a theoretical basis for explaining how some communities have governed common resources to ensure they remain viable for future generations. She showed that as long as certain rules are followed for the use and care of resources, there is no need for overly centralized command and control (by government) or by companies through privatization. Those rules for collective action included defining clear boundaries of the common resource, monitoring usage, informal conflict resolution and participatory structures for decision-making. Such rules could be very useful today to think about how to govern the data commons. This is critical given that people create data every time they 'click'. Data is created collectively, and is increasingly central to the ability of citizens to access their rights to education, health and services like public transport. Finding ways in which to make sure that we govern data creation to benefit the common good is thus central to the ability to govern inclusive growth. The mayor of Barcelona, Ada Colau, hired hackers in the city administration to set up a 'city data commons' to find ways for the city proactively to manage the data generated to improve public transport and social housing.

If we prioritize the economy's regenerative potential – that is, its ability to regenerate sources of value creation within both planetary boundaries and human and physical capital boundaries – it is useful to think in terms of a circular economy. As the Oxford economist Kate Raworth advocates, the circular economy not only minimizes waste, but also nurtures new institutions and collaborations between organizations and individuals so that we prosper while living within planetary boundaries. She argues that this requires investing in the areas that determine human flourishing such as food and housing, better working conditions, good health care and having a political voice, while ensuring that collectively we do not increase intolerably our pressure on the earth's life-supporting systems, such as a stable climate, fertile soils and a protective ozone layer.[44] Circular production and consumption of this kind disconnects economic growth from the extraction and consumption of materials, reducing resource dependency. As the Venezuelan-born economic historian Carlota Perez has written, this can spur economic and industrial renewal, with a related increase in investments in new types of services and methods of production.[45] Critically, it requires investment in the institutions that support human flourishing and planetary health, as the common-good perspective implies.

Participation: open systems to co-design our future

The moon landing was inspirational and required a massive collective effort: over 400,000 people across NASA, universities and the private sector contributed. But the mission itself came from a classic top-down initiative. Today's missions (as discussed in Chapter 5) require more citizen engagement in the vision of the mission itself – for example, who gets to define what a 'green city' might look like?

The philosopher Hannah Arendt developed the concept of the common good and public value – mentioned above – into an active participatory one with her concept of *vita activa*.[46] Her idea was that citizens should engage in public affairs, as this is the only way to escape totalitarianism and alienation in mass-production capitalism: here the idea of common good is reflected in the idea of an active citizen. But *vita activa* also means the need for society to be open to real debate, the contestation of ideas and explicit conflicts over values. For Arendt this was a good thing (as it was for ancient Greek political philosophy). Participation is not a silent, harmonious process. Economic theory, on the other hand, does not think about participation, which is left to those areas of political science focused on participatory institutions.

A great advocate of locally engaged citizens and the institutional structures that help them was Alexis de Tocqueville. In *Democracy in America* (1835) he identifies a key feature of American democracy as its participatory public and argues that this is the great strength of the American political system:

> It is extremely difficult to obtain a hearing from men living in democracies, unless it be to speak to them of themselves. They do not attend to the things said to them, because they are always fully engrossed with the things they are doing. For indeed few men are idle in democratic nations; life is passed in the midst of noise and excitement, and men are so engaged in acting that little remains to them for thinking. I would especially remark that they are not only employed, but that they are passionately devoted to their employments. They are always in action, and each of their actions absorbs their faculties: the zeal which they display in business puts out the enthusiasm they might otherwise entertain for idea.[47]

Alas, de Tocqueville's truths about America are under threat. As Robert Putnam puts it, 'declining electoral participation is merely the most visible symptom of a broader disengagement from community life. Like a fever, electoral abstention is even more important as a sign of deeper trouble in the body politic than as a malady itself. It is not just from the voting booth that Americans are increasingly AWOL.'[48] Nevertheless, we do increasingly see social movements having a large effect on how society develops in progressive ways – from the Fridays for Future (FFF) students fighting against the climate crisis to Black Lives Matter (BLM), which argues for a new social contract between races; but also, more widely, a renewed attention to all forms of inequalities and the investments and new structures needed to eliminate them.

The political scientist Ronald Inglehart argues that 'One frequently hears references to growing apathy on the part of the public ... These allegations of apathy are misleading: mass publics *are* deserting the old-line, oligarchical political organizations that mobilized them in the modernization era – but they are becoming more active in a wide range of elite-challenging forms of political action.'[49] Political consumerism, contentious activity, deliberative action and online participation have all increased since the halcyon days of the early 1960s. From this perspective, America is potentially witnessing a renaissance of democratic engagement rather than a general decline in participation.[50]

Participation requires reimagining the future together. For this reason, it is vital to bring different voices to the table, not only to react to a mission but to design it. Today, for example, labour unions are interacting with the green transition through the concept of the 'just transition', discussed in Chapter 5. But the real challenge is to make sure that the designing of missions crosses class boundaries. The reaction against the 'elite' is a wake-up call to the way in which many feel disenfranchised from the process of creation, having only to react to its consequences.

Finally, true participation requires systems to be open to change and adaptation based on the feedback received. Otherwise the participation — and feedback — is only tokenistic. Open-endedness must be a feature both of how systems are designed and how they work in practice. Open systems are more reactive to what can be seen as a counterveiling power, i.e. dissension. To avoid missions becoming the pet project of a minister or a tyrant, it is important to embed experimentation into the design of the system and to inform that experimentation — and learning from differences — from real participation. The European Union, for example, cannot dictate how cities become carbon-neutral: that must be discovered by the cities and their participants and organizations themselves.

Understanding systems change requires understanding the relationship between the parts and the whole. Complexity science looks at how the way in which agents (a fancy word for people!) interact in a system determines a macro structure (the surrounding environment) which feeds back to the micro (individual) interaction.[51] The lens of complexity theory, similar to the evolutionary approach to the economy inspired by the work of Joseph Schumpeter, emphasizes differentiation between the actors in a system and the competitive processes of selection which only allow some to grow. It also looks at how initial conditions (historical circumstances) might set a feedback loop that causes systems to 'lock in' and get stuck. This emphasis is different from the lens of mainstream economics, where the focus is not on differentiation but on average agents, and not on disequilibrium but on equilibrium and ideal outcomes. In the same way that complexity theory has greatly helped us in recent years to understand dynamic phenomena such as asset-price bubbles and crashes,[52] and system lock-in due to network effects, it can also help us understand ways in which public and private actors co-create change. Missions need to be open to uncertainty, while being able to carry out long-run planning and working across departments. Governments can fail to adapt to change due to their inability to take risks and welcome uncertainty, but especially their work within silos – closed to feedback loops. Open systems are full of uncertainty and ambiguity. And the more a system is participatory, the more it is open. Hence the more need there is to adapt to the underlying complexity.

Elsewhere I have summed up the dynamic capabilities that governments need to govern a market-shaping process in terms of ROAR.[53] ROAR is an acronym that stands for four key areas that can guide mission-oriented organizations:

- **R: Routes and directions:** setting a direction of change, which motivates innovation across different parts of the economy;
- **O: Organizations:** building decentralized networks of explorative organizations that can learn-by-doing and welcome trial and error, forming dynamic partnerships with private and third-sector partners;
- **A: Assessment:** evaluating the dynamic impact of market-creating investments, going beyond static cost–benefit analysis, and capturing the dynamic spillovers;
- **R: Risks and rewards:** forming symbiotic deals between public and private sectors so that both risks and rewards are shared.

Conclusion: Changing Capitalism

'If you want to build a ship, don't drum up people to collect wood and don't assign them tasks and work, but rather teach them to long for the endless immensity of the sea.'

Attributed to Antoine de Saint-Exupéry

After Neil Armstrong, Buzz Aldrin and Michael Collins returned from space in 1969, the astronauts were asked what it was like to feel their feet on the moon. Armstrong paused, and answered that it was humbling to see the earth from afar – and that it looked like an oasis in a sea of darkness. He said he was struck by the feeling that we had to learn to save and protect that oasis. He was talking not so much about climate change, but about the wars that were happening at the time in Vietnam and elsewhere. Buzz Aldrin said he was most struck by the way the moon landing was perceived on earth as a feat for all of humankind, as placards across the world said: '*We did it!*' He reflected that the space programme had to continue to foster that common feeling and common purpose – and that was perhaps its hardest challenge.

I am finishing this book during a defining moment in human history. The global population is grappling with one the worst health epidemics in modern times, protests over racial inequality are erupting across the world, and climate change is looming ever larger. It is clear that we can't wait any longer to do things differently and find a common purpose.

The status quo is failing too many people and changing the planet in ways that will also fail future generations. How can we do what Armstrong and Aldrin asked for: to protect people on our oasis, and to foster the common good?

This book has applied what I believe is the immensely powerful idea of a mission to solving the 'wicked' problems we face today. In it, I have argued that tackling grand challenges will only happen if we reimagine government as a prerequisite for restructuring capitalism in a way that is inclusive, sustainable and driven by innovation.

First and foremost, this means reinventing government for the twenty-first century – equipping it with the tools, organization and culture it needs to drive a mission-oriented approach. It also means bringing purpose to the core of corporate governance and taking a very broad stakeholder position across the economy. It means changing the relationship between public and private sectors, and between them and civil society, so they all work symbiotically for a common goal. The reason for the emphasis on rethinking government is simple: only government has the capacity to bring about transformation on the scale needed. The relationship between economic actors and civil society shows our problems at their most profound, and this is what we must unravel.

We can start by recognizing that capitalist markets are an *outcome* of how each actor in the system is organized and governed, and how the different actors relate to one another. This holds for the private and public sectors and for other sectors such as non-profits. No particular kind of market behaviour is inevitable. For example, the market pressure often cited as forcing a business to neglect the long term in favour of the short term, as too many companies do today, is the product of a particular organization of the market. Nor is there anything inevitable in government bureaucracies being too slow to react to challenges such as digital platforms and climate change. Rather, both are outcomes of *agency*, actions and governance structures that are *chosen* inside organizations, as well as the legal and institutional relationships between them. It is all down to design within and between organizations.

Capitalism is, indeed, in crisis. But the good news is that we can do better. We know from the past that public and private actors can come together to do extraordinary things. I have reflected on how, fifty years ago, going to the moon and back required public and private actors to invest, to innovate and to collaborate night and day for a common purpose. Imagine if that collaborative purpose today was to build a more inclusive and sustainable capitalism: green production and consumption, less inequality, greater personal fulfilment, resilient health care and healthy ageing, sustainable mobility and digital access for all. But small, incremental changes will not get us to those outcomes. We must have the courage and conviction to lift our gaze higher – to lead transformative change that is as imaginative as it is ambitious, aiming for something far more ambitious than sending a man to the moon.

To do this successfully, governments need to invest in their internal capabilities – building the competence and confidence to think boldly, partner with business and civil society, catalyse new forms of collaboration across sectors, and deploy instruments that reward actors willing to engage with the difficulties. The task is neither to pick winners nor to give unconditional handouts, subsidies and guarantees, but to *pick the willing*. And missions are about making markets, not only fixing them. They're about imagining new areas of exploration. They're about taking risks, not only 'de-risking'. And if this means making mistakes along the way, so be it. Learning through trial and error is critical for any value-creation exercise. Ambitious missions also have the courage to tilt the playing field.

If government is indeed a value creator that is driven by public purpose, its policies should reflect and reinforce that. Too many green policies today are just minor adjustments to a trajectory that still favours the old waste-prone behaviours and the financial casino that worsens inequality. A healthy economy that works for the *whole* of society must tilt the playing field consistently to reward behaviours that help us achieve agreed and desirable goals. That means achieving coherence in a multiplicity of fields, from taxes to regulation, from business law to the social safety net.

As emphasized throughout the book, it is key to not pretend that social missions are the same as technological ones. With challenges that are more 'wicked' it is essential that moonshot thinking is linked with support to underlying government systems. For example, a moonshot around disease testing or health priorities must interact closely with the public-health system, not replace or circumvent it. Similarly, a moonshot around clean growth must interact with transport systems and planning authorities and understand behavioural change. Thus it is critical to perceive missions not as siloed projects but as being intersectoral, bottom-up, and building on existing systems (such as innovation systems, among others).

Governments cannot pursue missions alone. They must work alongside purpose-driven businesses to achieve them.

As I've argued in this book, this requires addressing one of the biggest dilemmas of modern capitalism: restructuring business so that private profits are reinvested back into the economy rather than being used for short-term financialized purposes. Missions can accelerate this shift by shaping expectations about where business opportunities lie and also getting a better return for public investment. In this sense they can begin to walk the talk of stakeholder value. This means creating a more symbiotic form of partnership and collaboration in different sectors, whether in health, energy or digital platforms. A market-shaping perspective requires governing these interactions so that intellectual property rights, data privacy, pricing of essential medicines and taxation all reflect what needs to happen to reach the common objective. In health that must mean health innovation driven by the mission of better health care for all; in energy it must mean divestment from fossil fuels and the creation of public goods like green infrastructure and green production systems that protect the earthly oasis that Armstrong referred to; and in the digital domain it must mean the use of digitalization to improve the access of all people to the power of the technologies of the twenty-first century – while ensuring both data privacy and that our welfare states are strengthened, not weakened, by digital platforms.

Doing capitalism differently requires reimagining the full potential of a public sector driven by public purpose – democratically defining clear goals that society needs to meet by investing and innovating together. It requires a fundamentally new relationship between all economic actors willing and able to tackle complexity to achieve outcomes that matter.

These considerations make it necessary to go beyond the usual dichotomy between those advocating austerity (cuts in public spending) and those who argue that low interest rates and low demand require investment by any means necessary. Keynes famously said that in desperate times, digging a hole and filling it up again was better than doing nothing. And Galbraith also made a similar argument:

> For even when the state exercises artistically imperfect control over environment, the result will be better than when there is none at all. In the late twenties and early thirties the planners and architects of Washington DC swept clear an area between Pennsylvania and Constitution Avenues to build a vast block of buildings called the Federal Triangle. The Triangle is unimaginative, derivative and pretentious. Artists rightly condemned it. But it is far better than the cabbage patch of buildings it replaced. In its general cohesiveness it has come to be admired in comparison with those parts of the city where no similar effort was ever made.[1]

While Keynes was absolutely right to insist on counter-cyclical government investment, what mission-oriented policies add is the imagination necessary to decide where and how to invest, regardless of the business cycle. So instead of 'shovel-ready' investment in roads and houses, mission-oriented thinking frames the problems that green infrastructure can solve.

Mission-oriented thinking also requires being open to uncertainty and experimentation. As Roosevelt said in 1932: 'The country needs, and – unless I mistake its temper – the country demands bold, persistent experimentation. It is

common sense to take a method and try it: if it fails, admit it
frankly and try another. But above all, try something.'[2] Trying
'something' means taking risks, welcoming experimentation,
bringing vision and imagination to the role of active public
investment as Roosevelt did.

Reimagining also requires a new aesthetic. The period of
the Bauhaus in Germany between 1919 and 1933 tried to bring
a new aesthetic to everyday activities, combining the logic of
mass production with that of individual creativity. What now
are the aesthetics of a period of networked societies in which
there is rising inequality within regions as much as between
regions, yet massive potentials from new technologies to
interact more globally than ever? The question is critical if we
are to 'build back better' after any crisis, though the phrase
has been especially used during COVID-19.

Roosevelt's New Deal included not just bricks and cement
to build infrastructure. It put artists to work as part of the Federal Art Project (FAP), run by the Works Progress
Administration (later called the Work Projects Administration). FAP was not just a job programme, but a programme
to re-design and re-present public space. It employed large
numbers of artists, architects and designers to be involved in
the construction of public buildings, roads and other large-
scale works, and paid them a salary. The programme spanned
fine arts (e.g. murals and sculptures), practical art (e.g. post-
ers and stage sets) and educational services (e.g. galleries and
art centres). J. K. Galbraith too talked about the need to bring
a sense of beauty into public design. 'But far more than the
test of production, which is far too easy, the test of aesthetic
achievement is the one that, one day, the progressive community will apply.'

The green transition and the SDGs more widely also require a change in what we aspire to and how we achieve a good life, helping us to see as beautiful what was once seen as ugly – a large wind blade spinning on a green field – but also putting human experience at the centre of how we design public space. What is required is what Olafur Eliasson has called 'a new focus on experience and public space as a space where one feels safe to disagree'.[3]

The ideas in this book have been inspired by many. But it is probably significant that the previous chapter, looking at new theory, cites so many women scholars who have put life at the centre of the economy, not the economy at the centre of life: Hannah Arendt's work on the public life, *vita activa*; Elinor Ostrom's on creating community via the commons; Kate Raworth's on the construction of a circular economy which minimizes waste; Stephanie Kelton's on the power of long-run finance and an outcomes-based budgeting process; Edith Penrose's on the dynamic capabilities of value-creating organizations; Carlota Perez's on tilting the playing field towards a smart green transition. It is to the future young women scholars and practitioners that this book is also dedicated.

It is important to remember that change can only happen if we are convinced that a better life is possible. As the author Arundhati Roy wrote during the pandemic in 2020:

> Historically, pandemics have forced humans to break with the past and imagine their world anew. This one is no different. It is a portal, a gateway between one world and the next. We can choose to walk through it, dragging the carcasses of our prejudice and hatred, our avarice, our data

banks and dead ideas, our dead rivers and smoky skies
behind us. Or we can walk through lightly, with little lug-
gage, ready to imagine another world. And ready to fight
for it.[4]

I hope this book has given us some of the tools to imagine that
world and to fight the battles.

Notes

Preface

1 M. Mazzucato and R. Kattel, 'COVID-19 and Public Sector Capacity', *Oxford Review of Economic Policy*, 2020, https://doi.org/10.1093/oxrep/graa031

2 https://www.globalpolicyjournal.com/blog/09/04/2020/testing-capacity-state-capacity-and-covid-19-testing (accessed 20 April 2020).

3 https://www.theguardian.com/global-development/2020/apr/09/in-a-war-we-draw-vietnams-artists-join-fight-against-covid-19 (accessed 20 April 2020).

4 https://idronline.org/covid-19-and-lessons-from-kerala/ (accessed 29 May 2020).

5 https://www.technologyreview.com/2020/04/13/999313/kerala-fight-covid-19-india-coronavirus/?utm_medium=tr_social&utm_campaign=site_visitor.unpaid.engagement&utm_source=Twitter#Echobox=1588354761 (accessed 1 May 2020); M. Mazzucato and G. Quaggiotto, 'The Big Failure of Small Governments', https://www.project-syndicate.org/commentary/small-governments-big-failure-covid19-by-mariana-mazzucato-and-giulio-quaggiotto-2020-05 (accessed 17 July 2020).

6 https://www.wsj.com/articles/efficiency-isnt-the-only-economic-virtue-11583873155 (accessed 1 April 2020).

7 https://www.theguardian.com/commentisfree/2020/may/07/outsourcing-coronavirus-crisis-business-failed-nhs-staff (accessed 19 May 2020).

8 https://www.health.org.uk/news-and-comment/news/response-to-public-health-grant (accessed 15 July 2020).

9 https://www.health.org.uk/news-and-comment/news/response-to-public-health-grant (accessed 15 July 2020).

10 https://www.bma.org.uk/news-and-opinion/a-public-health-resurgence (accessed 15 July 2020).

11 https://www.theguardian.com/business/2013/dec/19/offender-electronic-tagging-serco-repay-68m-overcharging (accessed 15 May 2020).

12 https://www.forbes.com/sites/techonomy/2013/11/10/the-unhealthy-truth-about-obamacares-contractors/#c65b374644fd (accessed 1 June 2020); https://www.telegraph.co.uk/business/2018/06/06/serco-wins-670m-contract-us-healthcare-insurance/ (accessed 1 June 2020).

13 R. Davies, 'The Inside Story of the UK's NHS Coronavirus Ventilator Challenge' https://www.theguardian.com/business/2020/may/04/the-inside-story-of-the-uks-nhs-coronavirus-ventilator-challenge

14 See Alfred Schick for a review of how New Zealand has changed its approach to outsourcing due to lessons learned https://treasury.govt.nz/sites/default/files/2008-02/schick-rnzmo1.pdf (accessed 3 January 2020).

1. The Mission and Purpose

1 The text of Kennedy's speech can be found at https://er.jsc.nasa.gov/seh/ricetalk.htm

2 https://www.jfklibrary.org/events-and-awards/forums/past-forums/transcripts/50th-anniversary-of-the-missile-gap-controversy (accessed 13 July 2020).

3 https://www.planetary.org/space-policy/cost-of-apollo (accessed 7 September 2020).

4 https://euro1.safelinks.protection.outlook.com/?url=https%3A%2F%2Fwww.computer weekly.com%2Fnews%2F252466699%2FHow-Apollo-11-influenced-modern-computer-software-and-hardware&data=04%7C01%7C%7C535cfd17ce1f41f4e1b508d8960e9d70%7C1faf88fea9984c5b93c9210a11d9a5c2%7C0%7C0%7C637424336796749564%7CUnknown%7CTWFpbGZsb3d8ey JWIjoiMC4wLjAwMDAiLCJQIjoiV2luMzIiLCJBTiI6Ik1iha WwiLCJXVCI6Mn0%3D%7C1000&sdata=%2B9aa1O5Kyy wvzHZPUsB3ZYoeYZwWPVFbXGhzhxoG%2Byk%3D&r eserved=0 (accessed 11 2020).

5 J. K. Galbraith, *Economics and the Public Purpose* (Boston: Houghton Mifflin, 1973).

6 M. Mazzucato and R. Kattel, 'Getting Serious about Value', UCL Institute for Innovation and Public Purpose (IIPP PB 07, 2019) https://www.ucl.ac.uk/bartlett/public-purpose/publications/2019/jun/getting-serious-about-value

7 https://www.blackrock.com/americas-offshore/2018-larry-fink-ceo-letter

8 https://www.businessroundtable.org/business-roundtable-redefines-the-purpose-of-a-corporation-to-promote-an-economy-that-serves-all-americans

2. Capitalism in Crisis

1 L. Laybourn-Langton et al., 'This Is a Crisis: Facing up to an Age of Environmental Breakdown' (London: Institute for Public Policy Research, 2019) https://www.ippr.org/files/2019-11/this-is-a-crisis-feb19.pdf

2 UN Environment Programme, Emissions Gap Report 2019 https://www.unenvironment.org/resources/emissions-gap-report-2019

3 G. Ceballos, P. R. Ehrlich and R. Dirzo, 'Biological Annihilation via the Ongoing Sixth Mass Extinction Signaled by Vertebrate Population Losses and Declines', *PNAS*, 114 (30) (25 July 2017) https://doi.org/10.1073/pnas.1704949114

4 OECD, *Divided We Stand: Why Inequality Keeps Rising* (Paris: OECD Publishing, 2011) https://doi.org/10.1787/9789264119536-en

5 Figures represent weighted averages. See 'Decoupling of Wages from Productivity: What Implications for Public Policy?' in *OECD Economic Outlook*, 20 (2) (2018), pp. 51–65 https://www.oecd.org/economy/outlook/Decoupling-of-wages-from-productivity-november-2018-OECD-economic-outlook-chapter.pdf

6 T. Piketty and G. Zucman, 'Capital is Back: Wealth–Income Ratios in Rich Countries 1700–2010', *The Quarterly Journal of Economics*, 129 (3) (August 2014), pp. 1255–1310 https://doi.org/10.1093/qje/qju018

7 A. Tooze, *Crashed: How a Decade of Financial Crises Changed the World* (London: Allen Lane, 2018), Chapter 10.

8 IMF Global Debt Database, 2019, total stock of loans and debt securities issued by households and nonfinancial corporations as a share of GDP https://www.imf.org/external/datamapper/PVD_LS@ GDD/FADGDWORLD/USA/GBR/DEU/CHN/FRA

9 L. Dallas, 'Short-Termism, the Financial Crisis, and Corporate Governance', *Journal of Corporation Law*, 37 (2011), p. 264 https://papers. ssrn.com/sol3/papers.cfm?abstract_id=2006556; R. Davies et al., 'Measuring the Costs of Short-termism', *Journal of Financial Stability*, 12 (2014), pp. 16–25; J. Kay, *The Kay Review of UK Equity Markets and Long-term Decision Making* (2012) https://assets.publishing. service.gov.uk/government/uploads/system/uploads/attachment_ data/file/31544/12-631-kay-review-of-equity-markets-interim-report.pdf.

10 OECD and IMF data, cited in R. Fay, J.-D. Guenette, M. Leduc and L. Morel, 'Why Is Global Business Investment So Weak? Some Insights from Advanced Economies', *Bank of Canada Economic Review* (Spring 2017) https://www.bankofcanada.ca/wp-content/ uploads/2017/05/boc-review-spring17-fay.pdf

11 High Pay Centre, 2017, 'Executive Pay: Review of FTSE 100 Executive Pay Packages' http://highpaycentre.org/files/7571_CEO_ pay_in_the_FTSE100_report_(FINAL).pdf

12 Data and analysis from A. Haldane, 'Who Owns a Company?', speech at the University of Edinburgh, 22 May 2015, https://www. bankofengland.co.uk/-/media/boe/files/speech/2015/who-owns-a-company.pdf

13 https://www.theguardian.com/commentisfree/2020/may/28/ppe-testing-contact-tracing-shambles-outsourcing-coronavirus (accessed 1 June 2020); https://www.ft.com/content/e5079a62-4469-470d-af29-f79e82879853 (accessed 13 July 2020).

14 https://www2.deloitte.com/us/en/insights/economy/spotlight/ economics-insights-analysis-08-2019.html

15 https://www.federalreserve.gov/publications/files/2018-report-economic-well-being-us-households-201905.pdf

16 https://www.nytimes.com/2014/04/05/business/economy/ corporate-profits-grow-ever-larger-as-slice-of-economy-as-wages-slide.html (accessed 6 April 2020).

17 http://laborcenter.berkeley.edu/the-high-public-cost-of-low-wages/ (accessed 20 June 2020).

18 J. Ryan-Collins, T. Greenham, R. Werner and A. Jackson, *Where Does Money Come From?* (London: New Economics Foundation, 2012), p. 107.

19 O. Jordà, M. Schularick and A. M. Taylor, 'Macrofinancial History and the New Business Cycle Facts', *NBER Macroeconomics Annual*, 31 (1) (2017), pp. 213–63.

20 W. Lazonick, 'From Innovation to Financialization: How Shareholder Value Ideology Is Destroying the US Economy', in M. Wolfson and G. Epstein (eds), *The Handbook of the Political Economy of Financial Crises* (Oxford: Oxford University Press, 2013), pp. 491–511.

21 https://neweconomics.org/uploads/files/NEF_SHARE HOLDER-CAPITALISM_E_latest.pdf (accessed 9 July 2020).

22 J. Wood, 'Mortgage Credit: Denmark's Financial Capacity Building Regime', *New Political Economy*, 24 (6) (2019) https://www.tandfonline. com/doi/abs/10.1080/13563467.2018.1545755

23 https://www.marketwatch.com/story/airlines-and-boeing-want-a-bailout-but-look-how-much-theyve-spent-on-stock-buybacks-2020-03-18 (accessed 26 March 2020).

24 https://www.forbes.com/sites/stevedenning/2017/07/17/making-sense-of-shareholder-value-the-worlds-dumbest-idea/#15ba6 a722a7e (accessed 27 April 2020).

25 Private equity firms tend to raise debt to purchase the assets they invest in so as to minimize their initial equity requirement. Due to the leverage this entails, the investment strategy is often referred to as a 'leveraged buyout' (LBO).

26 https://www.theatlantic.com/magazine/archive/2018/07/toys-r-us-bankruptcy-private-equity/561758/ (accessed 14 May 2020).

27 Intergovernmental Panel on Climate Change, 2019, *Special Report, Global Warming of 1.5°C* https://www.ipcc.ch/sr15/

28 For the USA see https://www.eesi.org/papers/view/fact-sheet-fossil-fuel-subsidies-a-closer-look-at-tax-breaks-and-societal-costs (accessed 1 July 2020); and for Europe https://www.theguardian. com/environment/2019/jan/23/uk-has-biggest-fossil-fuel-subsidies-in-the-eu-finds-commission and https://eur-lex.europa.

eu/legal-content/EN/TXT/PDF/?uri=COM:2019:1:FIN& from=EN (accessed 10 September 2020).

29 https://www.edie.net/news/11/G20-nations-funnel-151bn-of-Covid-19-recovery-funding-into-fossil-fuels (accessed 30 November 2020).

30 P. B. Evans, *Embedded Autonomy: States and Industrial Transformation* (Princeton, NJ: Princeton University Press, 2012).

31 https://www.americanprogress.org/issues/general/news/2012/01/13/10976/obamas-government-reform-plan/ (accessed 24 April 2020).

32 https://www.reaganfoundation.org/ronald-reagan/reagan-quotes-speeches/news-conference-1/ (accessed 22 January 2020).

33 M. Mazzucato, *The Value of Everything: Making and Taking in the Global Economy* (London: Allen Lane, 2018).

34 W. Lazonick and M. Mazzucato, 'The Risk–Reward Nexus in the Innovation–Inequality Relationship: Who Takes the Risks? Who Gets the Rewards?', *Industrial and Corporate Change*, 22(4) (2013), pp. 1093–1128.

3. Bad Theory, Bad Practice:
Five Myths that Impede Progress

1 John Maynard Keynes, *General Theory of Employment, Interest, and Money* (London: Macmillan, 1936), p. 383.

2 R. M. Solow, 'Technical Change and the Aggregate Production Function', *The Review of Economics and Statistics*, 39 (3) (1957), pp. 312–20; P. M. Romer, *What Determines the Rate of Growth and Technological Change?* (Washington, DC: World Bank Publications, 1989).

3 N. Bloom and J. Van Reenen, 'Measuring and Explaining Management Practices across Firms and Countries', *The Quarterly Journal of Economics*, 122 (4) (2007), pp. 1351–1408; M. Mazzucato, *The Value of Everything: Making and Taking in the Global Economy* (London: Allen Lane, 2018). For a microeconomic theory of value see H. R. Varian, *Microeconomic Analysis* (New York: W. W. Norton, 1992). For a business strategy view of value creation in business see M. E. Porter, *Competitive Advantage: Creating and Sustaining Superior Performance* (New York : Free Press, 1985).

4 M. Mazzucato, *The Entrepreneurial State: Debunking Public Sector vs Private Sector Myths* (London: Penguin, 2018).

5 M. Angell, *The Truth about the Drug Companies: How they Deceive Us and What to Do about It* (New York: Random House, 2005); M. Mazzucato and G. Semieniuk, 'Financing Renewable Energy: Who is Financing What and Why It Matters', *Technological Forecasting and Social Change*, 127 (2018), pp. 8–22.

6 H.-J. Chang, *The Political Economy of Industrial Policy* (Basingstoke: Macmillan, 1994) and 'The Political Economy of Industrial Policy in Korea', *Cambridge Journal of Economics*, 17 (2) (June 1993), pp. 131–57 https://doi.org/10.1093/oxfordjournals.cje.a035227

7 J.-S. Shin, 'Dynamic Catch-up Strategy, Capability Expansion and Changing Windows of Opportunity in the Memory Industry', *Research Policy*, 6 (2017), pp. 404–16.

8 K. J. Arrow, 'An Extension of the Basic Theorems of Classical Welfare Economics', in J. Neyman (ed.), *Proceedings of the Second Berkeley Symposium on Mathematical Statistics and Probability* (Berkeley: University of California Press, 1951), pp. 507–32.

9 James M. Buchanan and Gordon Tullock, *The Calculus of Consent: Logical Foundations of Constitutional Democracy* (Ann Arbor: University of Michigan Press, 1962); D. C. Mueller, 'Public Choice: An Introduction', in C. K. Rowley and F. Scheider (eds), *The Encyclopedia of Public Choice* (New York: Springer, 2004), pp. 32–48.

10 J. Le Grand, 'The Theory of Government Failure', *British Journal of Political Science*, 21 (4) (1991), pp. 423–42.

11 C. Wolf, *Markets or Governments: Choosing Between Imperfect Alternatives* (Cambridge, MA: MIT Press, 1989).

12 J. W. Stiglitz and A. A. Weiss, 'Credit Rationing in Markets with Imperfect Information', *American Economic Review*, 71 (3) (1981).

13 J. M. Buchanan, 'Public Choice: Politics without Romance', *Policy: A Journal of Public Policy and Ideas*, 19 (3) (2003).

14 A. Innes https://blogs.lse.ac.uk/europpblog/2018/09/29/the-dismantling-of-the-state-since-the-1980s-brexit-is-the-wrong-diagnosis-of-a-real-crisis/ (accessed 2 January 2020).

15 J. E. Lane, *New Public Management: An Introduction* (London: Routledge, 2002).

16 C. Hood, 'The "New Public Management" in the 1980s: Variations on a Theme', *Accounting, Organizations and Society*, 20 (2–3) (1995), pp. 93–109.

17 https://www.wto.org/english/tratop_e/serv_e/symp_mar02_uk_treasury_priv_guide_e.pdf (accessed 9 July 2020).

18 https://www.nao.org.uk/wp-content/uploads/2018/01/PFI-and-PF2.pdf (accessed 1 May 2020).

19 *Financial Times*, 9 February 2018 https://www.ft.com/content/983c4598-0d88-11e8-839d-41ca06376bf2 (accessed 23 December 2019).

20 https://www.theguardian.com/society/2013/sep/18/nhs-records-system-10bn (accessed 22 January 2020).

21 https://www.instituteforgovernment.org.uk/publications/carillion-two-years (accessed 11 March 2020).

22 https://www.theguardian.com/business/2020/jan/15/carillion-collapse-two-years-on-government-has-learned-nothing (accessed 21 January 2020).

23 https://www.theguardian.com/society/2020/jan/17/two-hospitals-held-up-by-carillion-collapse (accessed 21 January 2020).

24 https://www.theguardian.com/business/2018/mar/07/carillion-bosses-prioritised-pay-over-company-affairs-mps-hear (accessed 21 January 2020).

25 J. Sekera, 'Outsourced Government – The Quiet Revolution: Examining the Extent of Government-by-Corporate-Contractor' (Economics in Context Initiative, 2017) http://www.bu.edu/eci/2017/09/27/outsourced-government-the-quiet-revolution-examining-the-extent-of-government-by-corporate-contractor/

26 United States Government Accountability Office, *Contracting Data Analysis; Assessment of Government-wide Trends*, March 2017, https://www.gao.gov/assets/690/683273.pdf

27 C. Hood and R. Dixon, *A Government that Worked Better and Cost Less? Evaluating Three Decades of Reform and Change in UK Central Government* (Oxford: Oxford University Press, 2015), cited in Abby Innes at https://blogs.lse.ac.uk/europpblog/2018/09/29/the-dismantling-of-the-state-since-the-1980s-brexit-is-the-wrong-diagnosis-of-a-real-crisis/ (accessed 2 January 2020).

28 https://fullfact.org/economy/rail-fares-inflation/ (accessed 28 April 2020).

29 https://orr.gov.uk/news-and-blogs/press-releases/2019/new-orr-rail-punctuality-statistics-will-help-industry-focus-on-boosting-performance-for-passengers (accessed 28 April 2020).

30 https://fullfact.org/economy/how-much-does-government-subsidise-railways/ (accessed 28 April 2020); https://neweconomics.org/2017/01/railways-failed-next (accessed 28 April 2020).

31 https://www.theguardian.com/world/2020/mar/23/covid-19-government-suspends-rail-franchise-agreements (accessed 2 July 2020).

32 https://www.ft.com/content/636d7f58-3397-11ea-a329-0bcf87a328f2 (accessed 2 July 2020).

33 See *Financial Times*, 29 January 2020, https://www.ft.com/content/636d7f58-3397-11ea-a329-0bcf87a328f2 (accessed 15 May 2020).

34 https://www.politico.com/story/2019/07/02/spies-intelligence-community-mckinsey-1390863 (accessed 14 July 2020).

35 P. Verkuil, *Outsourcing Sovereignty: Why Privatization of Government Functions Threatens Democracy and What We Can Do about It* (Cambridge: Cambridge University Press, 2007) doi:10.1017/CBO9780511509926

36 https://www.ingentaconnect.com/content/tpp/pap/2019/00000047/00000001/art00005;jsessionid=18599r8eh1s7s.x-ic-live-03 (accessed 14 July 2020).

37 Ibid.

38 https://publications.parliament.uk/pa/cm201617/cmselect/cmpubacc/772/77203.htm#_idTextAnchor004 (accessed 14 July 2020).

39 Finn Williams, 'Finding the Beauty in Bureaucracy: Public Service and Planning' (Lendlease, 2018) https://www.lendlease.com/uk/better-places/20180823-finding-the-beauty-in-bureaucracy/

40 Paul Hunter, *Guardian*, 1 April 2020 https://www.theguardian.com/commentisfree/2020/apr/01/why-uk-coronavirus-testing-work-catchup (accessed 1 April 2020).

41 https://www.washingtonpost.com/world/europe/how-mckinsey-quietly-shaped-europes-response-to-the-refugee-crisis/2017/07/23/2cccb616-6c80-11e7-b9e2-2056e768a7e5_story.html (accessed 31 August 2020).

42 https://www.vox.com/science-and-health/2019/12/13/21004456/bill
-gates-mckinsey-global-public-health-bcg (accessed 13 January 2020).

43 A. Laplane and M. Mazzucato, 'Socialising the Risks and Rewards of
Public Investments: Economic, Policy and Legal Issues', UCL Institute for Innovation and Public Purpose (IIPP WP 2019-09).

44 https://www.theguardian.com/world/2020/sep/18/covid-test-and
-trace-uk-compare-other-countries-south-korea-germany

45 https://www.theguardian.com/world/2020/oct/14/consultants-
fees-up-to-6250-a-day-for-work-on-covid-test-system

46 https://www.theguardian.com/politics/2020/sep/29/whitehall
-infantilised-by-reliance-on-consultants-minister-claims

47 https://www.americanrhetoric.com/speeches/sarahpalin2010tea-
partykeynote.html (accessed 1 July 2020).

48 A. Andreoni and H.-J. Chang, 'The Political Economy of Industrial
Policy: Structural Interdependencies, Policy Alignment and Conflict
Management', *Structural Change and Economic Dynamics*, 48 (1)
(2019), pp. 36–150.

49 As documented in K. Lee, C. Lim and W. Song, 'Emerging Digital
Technology as a Window of Opportunity and Technological Leap-
frogging: Catch-up in Digital TV by the Korean Firms', *International
Journal of Technology Management* 29 (1–2) (2005), p. 50: '[t]he whole
project was divided into digital signalling (satellite and terrestrial),
display (CRT, LCD, PDP) and ASIC chips (application-specific
integrated circuits chips, encoding, decoding, demultiplexer, display
processor). Each unit, GRI or private firm, was assigned to different
tasks with some intentional overlaps among them, namely two units
to undertake the same task to avoid the monopoly of the research outcomes. While each unit is supposed to share the results with other
firms, the private companies are observed to have tended to do
research on diverse aspects of the digital TV technology and to keep
important or core findings to themselves.'

50 Ibid.

51 United Nations Industrial Development Organization, 2020, 'Industrialization as the Driver of Sustained Prosperity' https://www.unido.
org/sites/default/files/files/2020-04/UNIDO_Industrialization_
Book_web4.pdf

52 http://www.civitas.org.uk/pdf/PickingWinners.pdf

53 https://www.nytimes.com/2020/07/01/opinion/inequality-goverment-bailout.html (accessed 4 July 2020).

54 http://www.civitas.org.uk/pdf/PickingWinners.pdf

55 https://www.theatlantic.com/technology/archive/2015/07/supersonic-airplanes-concorde/396698/ (accessed 3 July 2020); https://granttree.co.uk/concorde-a-soaring-tale-of-human-ingenuity/ (accessed 3 July 2020).

56 https://www.ati.org.uk/media/ufvdpces/ati-insight_13-spillovers.pdf; https://www.renishaw.com/en/heritage--32458 (accessed 3 July 2020).

57 M. Mazzucato and R. Kattel, 'Getting Serious About Value', UCL Institute for Innovation and Public Purpose (IIPP PB 07, 2019) https://www.ucl.ac.uk/bartlett/public-purpose/publications/2019/jun/getting-serious-about-value

58 https://ec.europa.eu/eurostat/databrowser/view/teina225/default/table?lang=en (accessed 3 January 2020); https://ec.europa.eu/eurostat/documents/2995521/9984123/2-19072019-AP-EN.pdf/437bbb45-7db5-4841-b104-296a0dfc2f1c (accessed 3 January 2020).

4. Lessons from Apollo: A Moonshot Guide to Change

1 The text of Kennedy's speech can be found at https://er.jsc.nasa.gov/seh/ricetalk.html

2 https://www.theguardian.com/science/2019/jul/14/apollo-11-civil-rights-black-america-moon

3 https://www.nasa.gov/centers/langley/news/factsheets/Rendezvous.html (accessed 1 January 2020).

4 https://history.nasa.gov/SP-4102.pdf (accessed 20 April 2020).

5 http://apollo11.spacelog.org/page/04:06:35:51/ (accessed 14 January 2020).

6 A. S. Levine, *Managing NASA in the Apollo Era* (Washington, DC: NASA Scientific and Technical Information Branch, special publication no. 4102, 1982).

7 A. Slotkin, *Doing the Impossible: George E. Mueller and the Management of NASA's Human Spaceflight Program* (Chichester: Springer-Praxis, 2012), p. 21.

8 Ibid., pp. 6, 42, 45.

9 Kranz's own account of his speech can be found at https://history.nasa.gov/SP-4223/ch6.html (accessed 28 April 2020).

10 M. Mazzucato, *Governing Missions in the European Union* (Luxembourg: European Commission, Directorate-General for Research and Innovation, 2019) https://ec.europa.eu/info/sites/info/files/research_and_innovation/contact/documents/ec_rtd_mazzucato-report-issue2_072019.pdf.

11 A 2018 article by NASA officials argued that the organization has exhibited several stages of organizational innovation during its history: https://hbr.org/2018/04/the-reinvention-of-nasa (accessed 10 June 2020).

12 Levine, *Managing NASA in the Apollo Era*, p. 271.

13 Ibid., p. 268.

14 P. Azoulay, E. Fuchs, A. P. Goldstein and M. Kearney, 'Funding Breakthrough Research: Promises and Challenges of the "ARPA Model"', *Innovation Policy and the Economy*, 19 (1) (2019), pp. 69–96.

15 https://lettersofnote.com/2012/08/06/why-explore-space/ (accessed 23 April 2020); Stuhlinger's letter was dated 6 May 1970.

16 http://college.cengage.com/history/ayers_primary_sources/king_justice_1966.html (accessed 23 April 2020).

17 https://www.nasa.gov/multimedia/imagegallery/image_feature_1249.html (accessed 1 September 2020).

18 It is unclear whether he made up the story about the count. Stuhlinger's story may be a parable rather than an historical account. https://www.reddit.com/r/history/comments/a5b8je/who_is_the_man_in_the_microscope_story_featured/

19 https://qz.com/1669641/innovations-from-apollo-11-mission-that-changed-life-on-earth/

20 https://www.jpl.nasa.gov/infographics/uploads/infographics/full/11358.jpg

21 Transcribed from a live video recording from the PBS documentary *Chasing the Moon* (2019), directed by R. Stone.

22 https://www.jfklibrary.org/archives/other-resources/john-f-kennedy-speeches/united-states-congress-special-message -19610525 (accessed 2 July 2020).

23 https://christopherrcooper.com/blog/apollo-program-cost-return-investment/ (accessed 26 March 2020).

24 https://www.usinflationcalculator.com/

25 Kennedy's Rice University speech: https://er.jsc.nasa.gov/seh/ricetalk.html

26 The blog of Christopher R. Cooper, 'Apollo Space Program Cost: An Investment in Space Worth Retrying?' https://christophercooper.com/blog./apollo-program-cost-return-investment/ (accessed 13 March 2020).

27 See Section 203(b)(5) of the 1958 National Aeronautics and Space Act https://history.nasa.gov/spaceact.html

28 House Committee on Science and Astronautics, 1964 NASA Authorization, 88th Cong., 1st sess. (1963), p. 3020.

29 W. M. Cohen and D. A. Levinthal, 'Absorptive Capacity: A New Perspective on Learning and Innovation', *Administrative Science Quarterly*, 35 (1) (1990), pp. 128–52.

30 Report to the President on Government Contracting for Research and Development, S. Doc 94, 87th Congress, 2nd Session, May 1962.

31 President Reagan Statement on Signing the Commercial Space Launch Act, 30 October 1984 http://www.presidency.ucsb.edu/ws/?pid=39335

32 L. Weiss, *America Inc.?: Innovation and Enterprise in the National Security State* (Ithaca, NY: Cornell University Press, 2014).

33 D. K. Robinson and M. Mazzucato, 'The Evolution of Mission-oriented Policies: Exploring Changing Market Creating Policies in the US and European Space Sector', *Research Policy*, 48 (4) (2019), pp. 936–48, https://www.sciencedirect.com/science/article/pii/S0048733318302373?via%3Dihub

5. *Aiming Higher: Mission-oriented Policies on Earth*

1 R. R. Nelson, 'The Moon and the Ghetto Revisited', *Science and Public Policy*, 38 (9) (2011), pp. 681–90.

2 J. D. Sachs, G. Schmidt-Traub, M. Mazzucato, D. Messner, N. Naki-
cenovic and J. Rockström, 'Six Transformations to Achieve the
Sustainable Development Goals', *Nature Sustainability* (September
2019) https://www.nature.com/articles/s41893-019-0352-9.pdf?
proof=trueMay

3 My first report for the European Commission was *Mission-oriented
Research and Innovation in the European Union: A Problem-solving
Approach to Fuel Innovation-led Growth* (Luxembourg: European Commission, Directorate-General for Research and Innovation, 2018)
https://publications.europa.eu/en/publication-detail/-/publication/
5b2811d1-16be-11e8-9253-01aa75ed71a1/language-en My second
report was on the governance of missions: *Governing Missions in the
European Union* (Luxembourg: European Commission, Directorate-
General for Research and Innovation, 2019) https://ec.europa.eu/
info/sites/info/files/research_and_innovation/contact/documents/
ec_rtd_mazzucato-report-issue2_072019.pdf

4 M. Miedzinski, M. Mazzucato and P. Ekins, 'A Framework for
Mission-oriented Innovation Policy Roadmapping for the SDGs',
UCL Institute for Innovation and Public Purpose Working Paper
(IIPP WP 2019-03). See p. 5 https://www.ucl.ac.uk/bartlett/
public-purpose/wp2019-03

5 https://assets.publishing.service.gov.uk/government/uploads/
system/uploads/attachment_data/file/664563/industrial-strategy-
white-paper-web-ready-version.pdf (accessed 2 July 2020).

6 Mazzucato, *Governing Missions in the European Union*.

7 See David Willetts, *The Road to 2.4%*, https://www.kcl.ac.uk/
policy-institute/assets/the-road-to-2.4-per- cent.pdf, pp. 26–8, and
Government Office for Science, *Raising Our Ambition Through Science*, 2019 https://assets.publishing.service.gov.uk/government/
uploads/system/uploads/attachment_data/file/844502/a_review_
of_government_science_capability_2019.pdf

8 https://www.ilo.org/wcmsp5/groups/public/---ed_emp/---emp_
ent/documents/publication/wcms_432859.pdf (accessed 13 March
2020).

9 European Commission, *Mission-oriented R&I Policies: Case Study
Report: Energiewende* (Luxembourg: European Commission,

Directorate-General for Research and Innovation, 2018) http://
europa.eu/!md89DM

10 http://fossilfritt-sverige.se/in-english/ (accessed 1 September
2020).

11 https://en.viablecities.se/om-viable-cities (accessed 1 September
2020).

12 https://www.london.gov.uk/sites/default/files/ggbd_high_
streets_adaptive_strategies_web_compressed_0.pdf

13 C. Leadbeater, 'Movements with Missions Make Markets', UCL
Institute for Innovation and Public Purpose (IIPP WP 2018-07)
https://www.ucl.ac.uk/bartlett/public-purpose/publications/
2018/aug/movements-missions-make-markets

14 M. Mazzucato, 'Mobilizing for a Climate Moonshot', Project Syndi-
cate, 2019 https://www.project-syndicate.org/onpoint/climate
-moonshot-government-innovation-by-mariana-mazzucato-2019-
10 (accessed 4 March 2020).

15 'A European Green Deal', European Commission, 11 December
2019, https://ec.europa.eu/info/strategy/priorities-2019-2024/
european-green-deal_en (accessed 12 December 2019).

16 *Politico*, 11 December 2019, https://www.politico.eu/article/the-
commissions-green-deal-plan-unveiled/ (accessed 12 December
2019)

17 https://www.markey.senate.gov/news/press-releases/senator
-markey-and-rep-ocasio-cortez-introduce-green-new-deal-
resolution

18 https://ec.europa.eu/info/sites/info/files/business_economy_
euro/banking_and_finance/documents/2020-sustainable-finance
-strategy-consultation-document_en.pdf

19 The work of behavioural economists builds on the writings of Herb
Simon, who used satisficing to explain the way in which people make
decisions with computational intractability and/or a lack of information, both of which preclude the use of mathematical optimization
procedures. Herbert A. Simon, 'Rational Choice and the Structure of
the Environment', *Psychological Review*, 63 (2) (1956), pp. 129–38.

20 M. Grubb, *Planetary Economics: Energy, Climate Change and the Three
Domains of Sustainable Development* (Abingdon: Routledge, 2014).

21 M. Mazzucato and M. McPherson, 'What the Green Revolution can Learn from the IT Revolution: A Green Entrepreneurial State', UCL Institute for Innovation and Public Purpose (IIPP PB 08, 2019).

22 C. Perez and T. M. Leach, 'Smart & Green. A New "European Way of Life" as the Path for Growth, Jobs and Well-being', in Council for Research and Technology Development (ed.), *Re-thinking Europe: Positions on Shaping an Idea* (Vienna: Holzhausen, 2018), pp. 208–23.

23 M. Mazzucato, G. Semieniuk and J. Watson, 'What Will it Take to Get Us to a Green Revolution?', SPRU, University of Sussex, 2015 https://www.sussex.ac.uk/webteam/gateway/file.php?name=what-will-it-take-toget-us-a-green-revolution.pdf&site=264

24 https://www.bmj.com/content/354/bmj.i4136

25 M. Mazzucato and V. Roy, 'Rethinking Value in Health Innovation: From Mystifications towards Prescriptions', UCL Institute for Innovation and Public Purpose (IIPP WP 2017-04) https://www.ucl.ac.uk/bartlett/public-purpose/publications/2018/jan/rethinking-value-health-innovation-mystificationstowards-prescriptions (accessed 10 September 2018).

26 National Institute for Health and Care Excellence, 'Sofosbuvir for Treating Chronic Hepatitis C', 2015, available at https://www.nice.org.uk/guidance/ta330/chapter/2-The-technology (accessed 18 September 2018).

27 Brad Loncar's blog (2018), available at https://www.loncarblog.com/sovaldi-and-harvoni-sales (accessed 18 September 2018).

28 https://www.bmj.com/content/370/bmj.m2661 (accessed 1 July 2020).

29 https://www.nytimes.com/1995/04/12/us/us-gives-up-right-to-control-drug-prices.html (accessed 10 July 2020).

30 https://fas.org/sgp/crs/misc/R44597.pdf, see p. 2 (accessed 17 July 2020).

31 https://www.healthaffairs.org/do/10.1377/hpb20171008.000174/full/ (accessed 17 July 2020).

32 https://www.thelancet.com/journals/lancet/article/PIIS0140-6736(05)71146-6/fulltext

33 https://www.bbc.co.uk/news/uk-england-london-18917932 (accessed 17 July 2020).

34 https://www.fastcompany.com/1682592/mind-the-gap-mapping-life-expectancy-by-subway-stop (accessed 6 June 2020).

35 See the *Guardian*, 4 June 2020 https://www.theguardian.com/commentisfree/2020/jun/04/covid-19-internet-universal-right-lockdown-online (accessed 6 June 2020).

36 https://www.fcc.gov/reports-research/reports/broadband-progress-reports/2019-broadband-deployment-report (accessed 17 July 2020).

37 https://www.ons.gov.uk/peoplepopulationandcommunity/householdcharacteristics/homeinternetandsocialmediausage/bulletins/internetaccesshouseholdsandindividuals/2019 (accessed 17 July 2020).

38 https://www.lloydsbank.com/assets/media/pdfs/banking_with_us/whats-happening/LB-Consumer-Digital-Index-2018-Report.pdf (accessed 17 July 2020) https://www.ons.gov.uk/peoplepopulationandcommunity/householdcharacteristics/homeinternetandsocialmediausage/bulletins/internetaccesshouseholdsandindividuals/2019 (accessed 17 July 2020).

39 https://www.weforum.org/agenda/2020/04/coronavirus-covid-19-pandemic-digital-divide-internet-data-broadband-mobbile/

40 See https://www.futurity.org/digital-divide-internet-access-pricing-2276962/ (accessed 17 July 2020); https://siepr.stanford.edu/sites/default/files/publications/20-001_0.pdf (accessed 17 July 2020).

41 European Commission (2020), Digital Economy and Society Index (DESI), available at https://ec.europa.eu/digital-single-market/en/scoreboard/italy

42 ISTAT (2019), Cittadini e ICT, *Statistiche Report* 18/12, available at https://www.istat.it/it/files//2019/12/Cittadini-e-ICT-2019.pdf

43 https://obamawhitehouse.archives.gov/the-press-office/2015/06/25/fact-sheet-connected-two-years-delivering-opportunity-k-12-schools (accessed 17 July 2020).

44 T. Blyth, *The Legacy of the BBC Micro: Effecting Change in the UK's Cultures of Computing* (London: Nesta, 2012).

6. Good Theory, Good Practice: Seven Principles
for a New Political Economy

1 http://newstoryhub.com/2019/04/it-will-take-cathedral-thinking-greta-thunbergs-climate-change-speech-to-european-parliament-16-april-2019/ (accessed 1 May 2020).

2 Conway, R. "How to be adaptive in government', UCL IIPP blog, https://medium.com/iipp-blog/purpose-driven-innovation-in-a-time-of-covid-19-296e9d05cb (accessed 1 July 2020).

3 J. K. Galbraith, *Economics and the Public Purpose* (Boston: Houghton Mifflin, 1973), p. 4.

4 See Chapters 8 and 9 in M. Mazzucato, *The Value of Everything: Making and Taking in the Global Economy* (London: Allen Lane, 2018).

5 Ibid.

6 B. Bozeman, *Public Values and Public Interest: Counterbalancing Economic Individualism* (Georgetown, Washington, DC: Georgetown University Press, 2007), p. 15.

7 W. M. Cohen and D. A. Levinthal, 'Absorptive Capacity: A New Perspective on Learning and Innovation', *Administrative Science Quarterly*, 35 (1) (1990), pp. 128–52.

8 https://www.project-syndicate.org/commentary/covid-vaccines-for-profit-not-for-people-by-mariana-mazzucato-et-al-2020-12

9 M. Mazzucato, R. Conway, E. Mazzoli, E. Knoll and S. Albala, 'Creating and Measuring Dynamic Public Value at the BBC', UCL Institute for Innovation and Public Purpose, Policy Report (IIPP WP 2020-16) https://www.ucl.ac.uk/bartlett/public-purpose/wp2020-16

10 M. Mazzucato and R. Kattel, 'Getting Serious About Value', UCL Institute of Innovation and Public Purpose (IIPP PB 07, 2019) https://www.ucl.ac.uk/bartlett/public-purpose/publications/2019/jun/getting-serious-about-value

11 E. Penrose, *The Theory of the Growth of the Firm* (Oxford, Basil Blackwell, 1959).

12 D. Teece, G. S. Pisano and A. Shuen, 'Dynamic Capabilities and Strategic Management', *Strategic Management Journal*, 18 (7) (1997).

13 M. E. Porter, *Competitive Advantage of Nations: Creating and Sustaining Superior Performance* (New York: Simon and Schuster, 2011).

14 As discussed in Chapter 2, the intellectual origins of such reforms can be traced back to the theory of public choice, as expounded by James M. Buchanan and Gordon Tullock in *The Calculus of Consent: Logical Foundations of Constitutional Democracy* (Ann Arbor: University of Michigan Press, 1962). For a critical overview see Wolfgang Drechsler, 'The Rise and Demise of the New Public Management', PAE Review, 2005 http://www.paecon.net/PAEReview/issue33/Drechsler33.html

15 W. M. Cohen and D. A. Levinthal, 'Absorptive Capacity: A New Perspective on Learning and Innovation', *Administrative Science Quarterly*, 35 (1) (1990), pp. 128–52.

16 R. R. Nelson and S. G. Winter, *An Evolutionary Theory of Economic Change* (Cambridge, MA: Harvard University Press, 1982).

17 All of the points made in this section are developed further in M. Mazzucato, *Governing Missions in the European Union* (Luxembourg: European Commission, Directorate-General for Research and Innovation, 2019) https://ec.europa.eu/info/sites/info/files/research_and_innovation/contact/documents/ec_rtd_mazzucato-report-issue2_072019.pdf and R. Kattel and M. Mazzucato, 'Mission-oriented Innovation Policy and Dynamic Capabilities in the Public Sector', *Industrial and Corporate Change*, 27 (5) (2018), pp. 787–801 https://doi.org/10.1093/icc/dty032

18 R. S. Lindner, S. Daimer, B. Beckert, N. Heyen, J. Koehler, B. Teufel, P. Warnke and S. Wydra, 'Addressing Directionality: Orientation Failure and the Systems of Innovation Heuristic. Towards Reflexive Governance', Fraunhofer ISI Discussion Papers *Innovation Systems and Policy Analysis* no. 52, 2016.

19 M. Grillitsch, B. Asheim and M. Trippl, 'Unrelated Knowledge Combinations: Unexplored Potential for Regional Industrial Path Development', Papers in Innovation Studies, Lund University, Center for Innovation, Research and Competences in the Learning Economy, 2017/10; OECD, *Systems Approaches to Public Sector Challenges. Working with Change* (Paris: OECD Publishing, 2017) http://dx.doi.org/10.1787/9789264279865-en.

20 A. Rip, 'A Co-evolutionary Approach to Reflexive Governance – and its Ironies', in J.-P. Voss, D. Bauknecht, and R. Kemp (eds), *Reflexive Governance for Sustainable Development* (Cheltenham, UK and Northampton, MA: Edward Elgar, 2006).

21 M. Mazzucato, R. Kattel and J. Ryan-Collins, 'Challenge-driven Innovation Policy: Towards a New Policy Toolkit', *Journal of Industry, Competition and Trade*, 1 (17) (2019) https://doi.org/10.1007/s10842-019-00329-w

22 https://www.youtube.com/watch?v=DNCZHAQnfGU&feature=youtu.be (accessed 17 July 2020)

23 The reasoning in this paragraph comes from S. Kelton, *The Deficit Myth: Modern Monetary Theory and the Birth of the People's Economy* (New York: Public Affairs, 2020).

24 W. Mosler, *Soft Currency Economics II: What Everyone Thinks That They Know About Monetary Policy Is Wrong* (Christiansted, USVI: Valance, 2012).

25 https://www.theguardian.com/world/2020/jun/22/britain-nearly-went-bust-in-march-says-bank-of-england (accessed 2 July 2020).

26 It should be noted that it is not so easy for developing countries with external debt in a currency other than their own to 'create' money. They need to use a mission-oriented approach to restructure their economies to reduce dependency on imports of essential goods and services such as food and energy. As long as they remain dependent on imports for those goods and services, then their own sovereign currency will also be dependent on the currency in which their external debt is denominated.

27 S. Kelton, 'As Congress Pushes a $2 Trillion Stimulus Package, the "How Will You Pay for It?" Question Is Tossed in the Trash', *The Intercept*, 27 March 2020 https://theintercept.com/2020/03/27/coronavirus-stimulus-package-spending/ (accessed 1 April 2020).

28 http://www.levyinstitute.org/publications/the-macroeconomic-effects-of-student-debt-cancellation (accessed 2 July 2020).

29 M. Deleidi and M. Mazzucato, 'Mission-oriented Innovation Policies and the Supermultiplier: An Empirical Assessment for the US Economy', forthcoming in *Research Policy*.

30 P. Quattrone, 'Accounting for God: Accounting and Accountability Practices in the Society of Jesus (Italy, XVI–XVII Centuries)', *Accounting, Organizations and Society*, 29 (7) (2004), pp. 647–83.

31 J. Hacker, 'How to Reinvigorate the Centre-Left: Predistribution' https://www.theguardian.com/commentisfree/2013/jun/12/reinvigorate-centre-left-predistribution (accessed 2 July 2020).

32 W. Lazonick and M. Mazzucato, 'The Risk–Reward Nexus in the Innovation–Inequality Relationship: Who Takes the Risks? Who Gets the Rewards?', *Industrial and Corporate Change*, 22 (4) (2013), pp.1093–1128.

33 M. Mazzucato, 'We Socialise Bailouts. We Should Socialise Successes, Too.' https://www.nytimes.com/2020/07/01/opinion/inequality-goverment-bailout.html (accessed 2 July 2020).

34 The US Must Take Equity Stakes in the Companies it Rescues', https://on.ft.com/37sfq8P via @FT (accessed 1 December 2020). And also this for background on the bigger topic: D. Detter, S. Föl-ster and J. Ryan-Collins, 'Public Wealth Funds: Supporting Economic Recovery and Sustainable Growth', UCL Institute for Innovation and Public Purpose, IIPP Policy Report (IIPP WP 2020-16), available at: https://www.ucl.ac.uk/bartlett/public-purpose/wp2020-16

35 All these are discussed in Chapter 8 of Mazzucato, *The Value of Everything*.

36 Ibid.

37 G. Charreaux and P. Desbrières, 'Corporate Governance: Stake-holder Value versus Shareholder Value', *Journal of Management and Governance*, 5 (2) (2001), pp.107–28.

38 https://www.statnews.com/2020/06/10/collective-intelligence-not-market-competition-deliver-best-covid-19-vaccine/ (accessed 1 July 2020).

39 W. J. Baumol, 'Entrepreneurship: Productive, Unproductive, and Destructive', *Journal of Business Venturing*, 11 (1) (1996), pp. 3–22.

40 https://www.latimes.com/business/la-fi-hy-musk-subsidies-20150531-story.html (accessed 1 April 2020).

41 https://astronomy.com/news/2018/12/despite-concerns-space-junk-continues-to-clutter-earth-orbit (accessed 13 March 2020).

42 https://www.project-syndicate.org/commentary/platform-economy-digital-feudalism-by-mariana-mazzucato-2019-10 (accessed 1 May 2020).

43 S. Zuboff, *The Age of Surveillance Capitalism: The Fight for a Human Future at the New Frontier of Power* (London: Profile Books, 2019).

44 K. Raworth, *Doughnut Economics: Seven Ways to Think like a 21st-century Economist* (White River Junction, VT: Chelsea Green Publishing, 2017).

45 C. Perez, 'Transitioning to Smart Green Growth: Lessons from History', in R. Fouquet (ed.), *Handbook on Green Growth* (Cheltenham: Edward Elgar, 2019), pp. 447–63.

46 H. Arendt, *The Human Condition* (Chicago: University of Chicago Press, 1958).

47 A. de Tocqueville (translated by R. Howard), *Democracy in America* (New York: J. & H. G. Langley, 1840).

48 Robert Putnam, *Bowling Alone: The Collapse and Renewal of American Community* (New York: Simon and Schuster, 2000), Chapter 2. Also Robert Putnam, *Our Kids: The American Dream in Crisis* (New York: Simon and Schuster, 2015); J. E. Leighley and J. Nagler, *Who Votes Now?* (Princeton, NJ: Princeton University Press, 2014).

49 Ronald Inglehart, *Modernization and Post-Modernization* (Princeton, NJ: Princeton University Press, 1997), p. 307; Russell Dalton, *The Good Citizen: How a Younger Generation is Reshaping American Politics* (2nd edn, Washington, DC: CQ Press, 2015), Chapter 4; Cliff Zukin et al., *A New Engagement?* (New York: Oxford University Press, 2006).

50 Dalton, *The Good Citizen*, Chapter 4; Zukin et al., *A New Engagement?*

51 W. B. Arthur, 'Complexity and the economy', *Science*, 284(5411) (1999), pp.107–9.

52 W. B. Arthur, 'Complexity in Economic and Financial Markets', *Complexity*, 1(1) (1995), pp. 20–25.

53 These questions are developed in M. Mazzucato 'From Market Fixing to Market-Creating: A New Framework for Innovation policy', special issue of *Industry and Innovation*: 'Innovation Policy – Can it Make a Difference?', 23 (2) (2016), and M. Mazzucato, 'Mission-oriented Innovation Policy: Challenges and Opportunities', *Industrial and Corporate Change*, 27 (5) (2018), pp. 803–15.

Conclusion: Changing Capitalism

1 J. K. Galbraith, *The New Industrial State* (Boston: Houghton Mifflin, 1967), p. 360.

2 https://georgiainfo.galileo.usg.edu/topics/history/related_article/ progressive-era-world-war-ii-1901-1945/franklin-d.-roosevelts- twenty-third-visit-to-georgia/fdr-oglethorpe-university -commencement-address-may-22-1932

3 Mark Godfrey (ed.), *Olafur Eliasson in Real Life* (London: Tate Publishing, 2019), p. 123

4 *Financial Times*, 3 April 2020 https://www.ft.com/content/10d8f5e8 -74eb-11ea-95fe-fcd274e920ca (accessed 2 July 2020).

Sources for Figures and Tables

— **Figure 1**: https://www.jpl.nasa.gov/infographics/uploads/info graphics/full/11358.jpg (accessed 16 September 2020).

— **Figure 2**: https://christopherrcooper.com/blog/apollo-program- cost-return-investment/ (accessed 13 March 2020).

— **Figure 3**: https://www.forbes.com/sites/alexknapp/2019/07/20/ apollo-11-facts-figures-business/#5fe0e34c3377 (accessed 2 July 2020).

— **Figure 4**: https://sdg-tracker.org/ (accessed 02 July 2020).

— **Figure 5**: The source for Figure 5 is the first report I wrote for the European Commission: M. Mazzucato, *Mission-oriented Research and Innovation in the European Union*, https://ec.europa.eu/info/sites/ info/files/mazzucato_report_2018.pdf, p. 11. The report eventually turned the mission idea into a new legal instrument for the Horizon Programme.

— **Figure 6**: https://ec.europa.eu/info/horizon-europe-next-research- and-innovation-framework-programme/missions-horizon-europe/ mission-boards_en (accessed 2 July 2020).

— **Figure 7**: Mazzucato, *Mission-oriented Research and Innovation in the European Union*, p. 22.

— **Figure 8**: Ibid., p. 240.

— **Figure 9**: The source for Figures 9 and 10 are the final report for the Commission for Mission-oriented Innovation and Industrial

Strategy. See p. 47 https://www.ucl.ac.uk/bartlett/public-purpose/sites/public-purpose/files/190515_iipp_report_moiis_final_artwork_digital_export.pdf (particular thanks to Dan Hill).

- **Figure 10:** Ibid. See p. 44 https://www.ucl.ac.uk/bartlett/public-purpose/sites/public-purpose/files/190515_iipp_report_moiis_final_artwork_digital_export.pdf (particular thanks to Dan Hill).

- **Figure 11:** Mazzucato, *Mission-oriented Research and Innovation in the European Union*, p. 26.

- **Figure 12:** This figure is sourced from a report I wrote for the Italian government on missions in Italy. https://www.ucl.ac.uk/bartlett/public-purpose/publications/2020/aug/mission-italia-investment-innovation-and-imagination, p. 38.

- **Table 1:** https://www.nasa.gov/sites/default/files/80660main_ApolloFS.pdf and https://spinoff.nasa.gov/flyers/apollo.html (accessed 2 July 2020).

- **Table 2:** https://www.planetary.org/space-policy/cost-of-apollo (accessed 7 September 2020).

- **Table 3:** M. Mazzucato, R. Conway, E. Mazzoli, E. Knoll and S. Albala, 'Creating and Measuring Dynamic Public Value at the BBC', UCL Institute for Innovation and Public Purpose, Policy Report (IIPP WP 2020-16), https://www.ucl.ac.uk/bartlett/public-purpose/wp2020-16.

- **Table 4:** M. Mazzucato, R. Kattel and J. Ryan-Collins, 'Challenge-driven Innovation Policy: Towards a New Policy Toolkit', *Journal of Industry, Competition and Trade*, 1 (17) (2019) https://doi.org/10.1007/s10842-019-00329-w.

Index

Abbey, George, 69
Abellio (transport operator), 39
Abernathy, Ralph, 62, 108
Acorn (company), 158
ACT UP (movement), 136
additionality, 180
Aerojet Rocketdyne, 64, 96, 97
Affordable and Clean Energy
    (SDG 7), 110
Agnew, Lord, 49
Airbus, 34
airline industry, 18
Aldrin, Buzz, 66, 90, 99, 204–5
Anders, William, 79
Apollo 1 disaster, 65, 68, 73–4
Apollo 7, 74
Apollo 8, 74, 79
Apollo programme: and computer
    technology, 82–4; controversy
    over, 62–3; cost, 3–4, 90;
    finance, 88–92, 181;
    innovation, 64–7; leadership,
    63–4; navigation system, 81–3;
    and organizational change,
    68–77; partnership with
    business, 93–102; public
    investment, 34, 60–1; risk-
    taking, 67; spillovers, 77–88;
    vision and purpose, 61–4
Arendt, Hannah, 199–200, 211

ARM Holdings, 158
Armed Forces Procurement Act
    (1947), 93
Armstrong, Neil, 66, 82, 90,
    204–5
ARPANET, 77
artificial limbs, 87
athletic shoes, 86
Attenborough, David, 131
Australia, 109

baby formula, 87
Bailey, Andrew, 185
Bain Capital, 18
Barker, Delia, 133
Bauhaus, Germany, 210
Bayh–Dole Act, 147
BBC Computer Literacy Project
    (1980s), 158
Beechcraft (Beech Aircraft), 97
Beijing Platform for Action from
    the Fourth World Conference
    on Women (1995), 111
Bell, David, 96
Benthamism, 170
Berners-Lee, Tim, 153
Biomedical Advanced Research
    and Development Authority,
    149
birth control pill, 136

237

238

About the Author

MARIANA MAZZUCATO, PHD, is a professor in the Economics of Innovation and Public Value at University College London, where she is the founding director of the UCL Institute for Innovation and Public Purpose. Her award-winning books include *The Entrepreneurial State: Debunking Public vs. Private Sector Myths* and *The Value of Everything: Making and Taking in the Global Economy.* She advises policymakers worldwide and is a member of the South African Presidential Economic Advisory Council, the Scottish government's Council of Economic Advisers, the United Nations Committee for Development Policy, and the OECD's Secretary General's Advisory Group on a New Growth Narrative. She is also a special adviser to the Italian prime minister and the European Commissioner for Research, Science, and Innovation. She has won many prizes, including the 2018 Leontief Prize for Advancing the Frontiers of Economic Thought and the 2020 John von Neumann Award. She lives in London with her husband and four children.